WRITERS AND T

ISOBEL ARMS
General Ec

BRYAN LOUC
Advisory E

Dorothy Richardson

DOROTHY RICHARDSON

Dorothy Richardson

Carol Watts

Northcote House

in association with
The British Council

First published in 1995 by Northcote House Publishers Ltd, Plymbridge House, Estover Road, Plymouth PL6 7PZ, United Kingdom.
Tel: (01752) 735251. Fax: (01752) 695699.

British Library Cataloguing-in-Publication Data
A catalogue record for this book is available from the British Library

ISBN 0 7463 0708 X

Typeset by PDQ Typesetting, Stoke-on-Trent
Printed and bound in the United Kingdom by BPC Wheatons Ltd, Exeter

Contents

for Elaine

Acknowledgements

This has been an enjoyable book to write. I would like to thank colleagues for making it so – especially Isobel Armstrong, for her enthusiasm and support, and Laura Marcus, with whom I have thought about and taught the Dorothy Richardson–Virginia Woolf debate. Students on the Birkbeck 'Women and Modernism' course have also contributed greatly to this exchange. Joanne Winning, whose own work on Richardson will open up new perspectives, has generously shared her material as well as her practical skills during time as a research assistant on this project, for which I am very grateful. As always, I owe the biggest debt of thanks to John Kraniauskas.

Biographical Outline

Dorothy Richardson was born in Abingdon, Berkshire, in 1873. She spent her early years there, eventually moving with her family to Putney in the suburbs of London. In 1891, at 17, Richardson went to Hanover, Germany, to work as a governess. She returned after six months to take up other governessing positions in North London and the Home Counties. In 1893 her father was bankrupted. Her mother's mental health suffered an irreparable blow at this time and, during a recuperative trip to Hastings with the 22-year-old Dorothy, she committed suicide.

Richardson moved to Bloomsbury in 1896 to work as a dental receptionist. Here, with limited financial resources, she entered the intellectual and political melting-pot of *fin-de-siècle* London. During this period she met three people who were greatly to influence her emotional life. On her arrival she met Benjamin Grad, a Russian–Jewish emigré. In 1896 Richardson met H. G. Wells, whose wife was an old school friend. She began a brief affair with Wells which was to end in pregnancy and a miscarriage in 1904. In 1906 she met Veronica Leslie-Jones, the 'Amabel' of *Pilgrimage*, and published her first review in *Crank: An Unconventional Magazine* in the same year. At the height of the emotional complications which existed between the two women, Richardson orchestrated an engagement between Leslie-Jones and her ex-lover, Grad, which was to result in their marriage in 1908. Richardson retreated to Vaud in Switzerland, where she suffered a nervous breakdown. On her return, Richardson spent some time on the farm of a Quaker family, who were to become the 'Roscorlas' of her novel. In 1912 she began work on *Pointed Roofs*, the first of the *Pilgrimage* series, which was published in 1915 by Duckworth. The writing of *Pilgrimage* became her life's work.

In 1923 Richardson met Winifred Bryher and H.D. (Hilda Doolittle), and through this connection started to write a regular column on film for *Close Up* in 1927. In 1917 she had married the artist Alan Odle, and they divided their time between Cornwall and London until his death in 1948, supported by her translation and journalistic work, and by the generosity of Bryher. Richardson continued the writing of *Pilgrimage*, despite failing eyesight and constant financial difficulty, until 1954. She died in a nursing home in Beckenham in 1957, unknown to staff and public. Her insistence that she was a writer was regarded as a sign of senile delusion until a visiting friend confirmed its truth. *March Moonlight*, the unfinished novel in the *Pilgrimage* series, was published posthumously in 1967. Dorothy Richardson is buried in Streatham Park Cemetery, London.

Abbreviations

The Virago edition of *Pilgrimage* (4 vols.; London, 1979) has been used throughout, cited in the text as volume number followed by page number.

The following abbreviations have been used in citing other works by Richardson:

B.   'Beginnings' (1933), in *Journey to Paradise*, ed. Trudi Tate (London: Virago, 1989), 110-13

CBP   'Mr Clive Bell's Proust', *New Adelphi*, 2/2 (1929), 160-2

CU1   'Continuous Performance', *Close Up*, 1/1 (1927), 34-7

CU2   'Continuous Performance: The Increasing Congregation', *Close Up*, 1/6 (1927), 61-5

CU3   'Continuous Performance', *Close Up*, 2/3 (1928), 51-5

CU4   'Continuous Performance: The Thoroughly Popular Film', *Close Up*, 2/4 (1928), 44-50

CU5   'Continuous Performance: Pictures and Films', *Close Up*, 4/1 (1929), 51-7

CU6   'Continuous Performance: Dialogue in Dixie', *Close Up*, 5/3 (1929), 211-18

CU7   'Continuous Performance: A Tear for Lycidas', *Close Up*, 7/3 (1930), 196-202

CU8   'Continuous Performance: Narcissus', *Close Up*, 8/3 (1931), 182-5

CU9   'Continuous Performance: This Spoon-Fed Generation?', *Close Up*, 8/4 (1931), 304-8

CU10   'Continuous Performance: The Film Gone Male', *Close Up*, 9/1 (1932), 36-8

G.   'The Garden' (1924), in *Journey to Paradise*, ed. Trudi Tate (London: Virago, 1989), 21-4

WF   'Women and the Future', *Vanity Fair*, 22 (1924), 39-40

Note on the Text

Richardson often uses unusual punctuation such as ellipsis to indicate the impressionistic flow of her protagonist's consciousness. All such stops appearing in quotations are her own, unless they are in square brackets, when they signal an omission of part of the text.

Prologue

How long
Do works endure? As long
As they are not completed.

Bertolt Brecht

Dorothy Richardson is one of the major novelists of the twentieth century, comparable in stature to Proust, Joyce, and Woolf. She was reputed to have influenced more writers in her heyday than any other author. Yet by the time of her death in the late 1950s she had been largely forgotten. Her life's work, a thirteen-volume sequence of a novel, *Pilgrimage*, had been all but lost. Now times have changed. With its republication by Virago in four volumes, and a growing critical interest, Richardson's novel is offering a challenge to the clubbish confines of literary modernism, and finding new readers.

This book is an exploration of Richardson's extraordinary novel. It does not read the writer's life into her work, since her biographer, Gloria Fromm, has already suggested how this might be done. Rather it looks at how *Pilgrimage*'s representation of a life of a woman from the 1890s to the time of the First World War becomes a measure of a much wider issue: the experience of modernity itself. Like Proust's great novel, *Pilgrimage* goes in search of lost time: but it does so in order to reveal dimensions of the historical phenomenon of women's experience, suddenly broken out from the restraint of tradition as 'something new – a kind of different world'. As such the novel continues to speak to the contemporary reader, offering a form of cultural memory of a difficult coming-to-consciousness, a struggle over gendered meanings and identities which is no less contested today.

1

Why do works like *Pilgrimage* disappear? In some ways their rough ride through time is a revealing statement about the interaction of all literary texts with any given moment. For me, though, Richardson's novel is a rather special case, because it is a text that dares to be unfinished in a radical sense: it aims to make its aesthetic experiment answerable, open, to the social conditions in which a woman finds herself, in ways that aestheticist high modernism found difficult to countenance. In my reading of the novel I will explore how I think *Pilgrimage* achieves this – examining the form of cultural memory it enacts, the city spaces it explores, and finally its interaction with the medium of film as a means of imagining that utopian space – a women's public sphere – as the very sign of their historical experience of the new.

1

Continuous Performance

Each generation experiences itself as a break away from the traditions that have preceded it. For the generation coming of age during the First World War, the necessity of this modernist gesture must have been of a different order. This was a generation that was to be 'lost' and traumatized on the field of battle, that was witness to sudden transformations in the roles of the sexes and the reward of the women's vote, in an age that had already begun to valorize the new. It was a generation too that would see itself moving on film, in a world prepared to re-stage wars and revolutions for the camera. Subject to the demands of a rapidly changing and uncertain environment and yet to the equally shocking stasis, arrestation, of wartime: how was such a generation to define itself except through negation, against the certainties of a time it could barely remember?

The writer Winifred Bryher, remembering 1916:

> It was a moment when normal adolescence ceased, and although the suppression was accepted, it was a violently imposed external barrier and actual impulses made themselves felt in a hidden way, through delight in small events that made the days endurable or despair that was as old and barren as the press communiques at night. There were food queues, there was no heat in winter-damp rooms. Against this cold, and never ending anxiety, a searchlight swung in black sky. Into this suspended moment came *Pilgrimage*.[1]

Dorothy Richardson, author of *Pilgrimage*, was not of this generation. Born in 1873 to a family who aspired to the genteel life-style of the Home Counties English middle class, she had been educated to expect the leisure and security of her status, and to use her mind. Her own break with late-Victorian tradition had come rather abruptly with the bankruptcy of her father in the 1890s, when she had found independent employment for herself in central

London. By the time of the publication of the first volume – the first of thirteen – of *Pilgrimage, Pointed Roofs*, in 1915, Dorothy Richardson was already in her early forties, and the author of a number of journalistic articles as well as an accomplished translator. She was self-avowedly a pre-war writer, though *Pilgrimage* was to occupy her until the 1950s. For some, such as her friend John Cowper Powys, who wrote about her work with hyperbolic enthusiasm, it would always be the critics of her own generation – 'older, calmer and more self-possessed' than those who shared the 'raw, scoffing, unhappy, defeatist mood of after-war writers' – who would best understand her.[2]

Yet Bryher's encounter with *Pilgrimage* in the dark years of the war argues differently. 'Reading *Pointed Roofs* and *Backwater*,' she wrote, 'not one but many, were able to resume for a few hours, the growth proper to their age. It was not escape, but an actual sense of movement.'[3] Richardson's close exploration of the consciousness of an adolescent protagonist, Miriam Henderson – embarked on 'an adventure so searching and, sometimes, so joyous as to produce a longing for participation', as she described in her later Foreword (i. 10) – evidently bridged an experimental gap, allowing readers to reassume a development that circumstances had refused them. From *Pointed Roofs*, set in 1890, when the 17-year-old Miriam Henderson leaves for a teaching job in Germany, to her struggles as an emergent 'new woman' in London, and her mature reflection in later volumes, *Pilgrimage* insistently records, with an obsessive eye for detail and nuance, the changing thoughts, memories, and desires of a woman living an ordinary life at the turn of the twentieth century. Through Miriam's search for freedom from the Victorian conformity that produced her, the reader also might experience in gentler ways, as Bryher described it, 'the slow progression from the Victorian period to the modern age'.[4]

Lawrence Hyde, writing in the *Adelphi* in 1924, at a loss to understand what Richardson was attempting, argued that to describe Miriam's life in terms of 'growth' was inappropriate:

> growth implies synthesis of experience, and throughout the work Miriam receives impressions far faster than she can deal with them. She serves principally as a delicate and efficient receiving instrument, a medium through whom we can look at life so surely and clearly that we forget that she is there between us and the pictures which are presented to us, forget even that the pictures are ostensibly only there because of the effect which they had on *her*.[5]

4

Richardson's failure, the article suggested, is that the reader is not given a vantage-point, 'a certain serenity', from which to make sense of the 'raw material' collected in her narrative.[6] Richardson's method, which May Sinclair had termed in 1918, for the first time in critical discourse, a 'stream of consciousness', appeared to lack both form and design.[7] Moreover, it brought the reader up against images and impressions without, seemingly, a means of framing them. The problem was one of lack of distance, and also (for some) superficiality: however sensitive the registering of 'tiny signals – shades of expression on people's faces, sudden similarities which are sensed between things widely separated on the surface, unsuspected identifications', Miriam, Hyde argued, remains on that surface 'without any laceration', unable to penetrate to a deeper truth, to 'plunge into life'.[8]

It may be that Richardson's exclusive focus on Miriam's 'damned egotistical self', as Virginia Woolf put it, was less of an obstacle to the narcissism of an adolescent reader in 1916.[9] Woolf shared, with other critics, many of Hyde's reservations about Richardson's narrative. But it may also be true that *Pilgrimage* captured and represented a particular mode of experience – that of the impact of modernity on an individual life – which spoke to a wartime generation suddenly accelerated, fragmented, lost, new. In this sense the adolescence that is suggested in the limits of Miriam's consciousness represents a diagnosis of the broader condition of English culture of the time. But what would it mean to ask this generation to plunge deeper, to acknowledge its trauma with serenity, to reaffirm those universal truths now surely in question, when the surface was itself a place of kaleidoscopic experience and even a last refuge?

In Rebecca West's *The Return of the Soldier*, published in 1918, something resembling this question is posed. A soldier returns from the front, suffering from shell-shock and amnesia, having shut out the last fifteen years of his life. All he can recall are the idyllic days of his youth and the young woman he had loved, now married and 'furred with neglect and poverty', but to him as youthful as ever. His own wife means no more to him than another guest in the same hotel. The soldier exists in a present suddenly become insubstantial, in a palpable past which is no longer accessible. Those around him are at once youthful and yet, seeing themselves through his eyes, disturbingly aged. He moves through his grand house, now modernized, as if using a map from the past, 'loose limbed like a boy'. Finally there has to be a choice, taken selflessly by his first love: either to bring about his return to face his trauma, or to allow him to enjoy this 'magic circle' where he would nevertheless 'not be quite a man'. The memory of the death of his baby son shocks him into the present, his body stiffening in its recollection. The choice made in *The Return of the Soldier* is for a kind of bitter adulthood, an acknowledgement of loss and shared trauma, a facing out of the trenches which have invaded 'the dreams of Englishwomen to-day'.[10] It is also to leave the past behind.

West's novel points to a wider historical dilemma brought into relief by the war, as if by an extreme symptom: how to remember, whether to forget. To many the First World War signalled the end of a golden epoch, for others it was the last gasp of an age that had been dying fitfully for more than a decade. In Thomas Mann's *The Magic Mountain* it is only from the removal of a mountain sanatorium that the gulf of time which is life before the war can be surveyed and the sickness diagnosed; Hans Castorp's final entry into society, expected of a hero of a *Bildungsroman*, is his active service in the blind and muddy lowlands at the Front. D. H. Lawrence's novel of 1916, *Women in Love*, repressed the war but explored the brittle violence and freedom released in a perceived waning of tradition as a personal and cultural crisis, ending in those mountain wastes.

This sense of an ending seems to be wholly lacking from Richardson's *Pilgrimage*, a project that was to last all her life and which she refused to bring to a close. Yet the novel is importantly an act of cultural memory, and even as it re-creates the years of a young woman's life between 1891 and 1912, it is shaped by the conditions of its telling.

Pilgrimage has to be thought in this double sense, like a fold in time, a continual performance of recording and recognition which is as much marked by the 'tiny signals' and 'unexpected identifications' of its present as those of the pre-war, *fin-de-siècle* world it evokes. What would such an affirmative portrayal of the Germany of 1890 mean in the Hun-hating years of the First World War? How would Miriam Henderson's experiences and allegiances in the London of anarchists and revolutionaries look to those voting in the first Labour government after the war, in the years of the Red Scare? Where would a new woman of the 1890s find herself, twenty years and more later? And how would it

6

become possible to write in anti-Semitic form of Jews and Jewishness, of Germany, in the following decades, with evident knowledge of and opposition to the rise of Fascism? The novel brings a memorializing pressure to bear on a life in which each thought and sensation become significant because ephemeral, because they have once been lived.

'Consciousness comes into being at the site of a memory trace,' Freud wrote.[11] In *Pilgrimage* the consciousness of Miriam Henderson takes place in precisely this sense. Yet, for all its idiosyncratic individuality, that trace is also representative in cultural terms: an accumulation of material, half-unworked, part unconscious, registered, but not, as the critics pointed out, synthesized. In what remains of this first chapter I want to explore the folded narrative of *Pilgrimage* as an act of memory: first by considering Miriam's journey to Germany in *Pointed Roofs*, then by noting Richardson's encounter with Proust, and finally by exploring the specific technologies of memory at work in the narrative.

THE SIGNIFICANCE OF GERMANY

Pilgrimage opens with a leave-taking, a train journey to Hanover, and the prospect of a job as an English teacher in a German girls' school. Saratoga trunk packed, Miriam Henderson thus begins her passage to independence, positioned in a novelistic tradition which includes Charlotte Brontë's *Villette*. Richardson had completed *Pointed Roofs* in 1913; to write in such positive terms about 'das deutsche Vaterland – Germany, all woods and mountains and tenderness' (i. 21), however sanctioned by autobiographical verity, seems an interesting choice at this time.[12]

Or at least a revealing one. It provides us with one of many maps with which to make sense of the dimensions of this narrative. Miriam's removal to Germany is about 'escape', about gaining a distance from which to see England all the more clearly. Germany is in part a state that Miriam 'achieves' (i. 66), unlike provincial England synonymous with high European culture: Beethoven, Schiller, Goethe. Yet it is also a rival. However much Miriam is transported by the idyllic scenes of burgher towns, with their 'high quiet peaked houses, their faces shining warm cream and milk-white, patterned with windows' (i. 115), she is, despite herself, continually drawn to make comparisons. The girls at the school are grouped in her mind according to national characteristics: of physiognomy, of manner, of dress, of handwriting. At times the accessible foreignness that Germany opens up to her is a source of excitement, offering her confirmation, the prospect of transformation, in its estrangement: 'she imagined all their people looking in and seeing them so thoroughly at home in this little German restaurant, free from home influences, in a little world of their own' (i. 88). Yet there remains something unrecuperable about German difference: the 'opaque blue glass' (i. 167) of the eyes of a Prussian soldier; the male farmworkers who trouble her – 'They looked up with strange eyes. She wished they were not there' (i. 114).

On one level Germany makes available to Miriam a space in which both she and the reader can begin to make out the shape of her desires, the limitations of her self-knowledge. In this arena of reassuring European otherness she can play out the attractions of conformity and difference that will mark her in complex ways throughout the narrative of *Pilgrimage*. On another level Germany offers at certain moments a particular mode of experience – aesthetic, contemplative, epiphanic – that she will recall and relive in later volumes, most significantly in the Swiss mountains of *Oberland*.

Yet the opening move to Germany is more central to *Pilgrimage* than this. In the light of the whole work *Pointed Roofs* might appear strangely disconnected as an opening, less experimental and complex than the following volumes, though none the less a formal departure for the novel in 1915. However, it sets up a particular context in which Germany is assessed as a rival culture. This context is one of imperial competition, a fact of which Miriam is not unaware, even in *Pointed Roofs*. Her own modern education, she points out, had made her 'troubled about the state of Ireland and India' (i. 81). The serenity of German life is both attractive and yet also in some sense suspect, a mask from which strange, 'evil' eyes suggest another, inexplicable motivation.

Like the German culture of Forster's *Howards End*, which represents both a base, aggressive materialism and a dreamy idealism, Miriam's Germany contains both elements. At times *Pointed Roofs* exhibits an anti-xenophobic concern to represent Germany through the 'kind of therapeutic liberal tolerance and self-critique' that Fredric Jameson finds in *Howards End*.[13] Yet

8

Miriam also registers a militarism which, from the hindsight of 1913, after more than a decade of invasion scares, is becoming deeply significant. The retrospection of the narrative invests the most innocent and unconscious of details – the church congregation described, for example, as a 'little army' (i. 76) – with meaning. In later volumes, written after the war and during the build-up of German Fascism (set in the late 1890s and the early years of the twentieth century), Germany emerges more evidently as a threat, through the discussions Miriam has of contemporary political debates. Most often she is assessing the views of others: Reich, a Hungarian commentator; or the opinions of her English employer, who likes to sing 'Gunga Din', on the Boer War. England, 'as a good colonist', is said to be the European inheritor of the Roman Empire, 'spreading and conquering, making Empire and Law' (iv, 200). Its strength is seen to be in its cosmopolitan diversity, as Reich argues:

> England has attracted thousands of brilliant foreigners, who have made her, including the Scotch, who until they became foreigners in England were nothing. And the foreigner of foreigners is the permanently alien Jew. [...] Countries without foreigners are doomed. Like Hungary. Doomed to extinction if England does not beat Germany. (iii. 376)

'The remark "England and Germany are bound to fight" renders the war more likely each time that it is made, and is therefore made the more readily by the gutter press of either nation,' observes the narrator of *Howards End*.[14] 'That war can be written away; by journalists and others, written into absurdity', argues Miriam's companion Hypo Wilson – a fictionalized H. G. Wells (iii. 376). Miriam Henderson reserves her judgement, 'scattered', in the words of her companion: 'There are so many opinions, and reading keeps one always balanced between different sets of ideas' (iii. 377). By positioning her protagonist in the midst of a density of impressions and opinions and refusing her the comfort or detachment of synthesis, Richardson conveys what it means to live out a life in historical terms. Could it be, Miriam asks herself in hyperbolic tones, as her dentist employer packs absorbents into a patient's mouth, *'that my assignation with to-morrow's dawn owes its security to Dreadnoughts?'* (iv. 203).

The first volume of *Pilgrimage* thus locates late-Victorian/

Edwardian England in terms of a geography which is 'the ground symphony of history' (iii. 376). Miriam's experiences in London will be that of a metropolitan individual, one who lives out her life at the centre of an imperial nation-state. To begin this epic project looking in at English life from an outside is to comment on the insufficiency of such a life, the 'troubling' nature of what lies beyond (but also within) its borders. As Fredric Jameson has put it, in the imperialist system:

> daily life and the existential experience in the metropolis – which is necessarily the very content of the national literature itself, can no longer be grasped immanently; it no longer has its meaning, its deeper reason for being, within itself. As artistic content it will always have something missing about it, but in the sense of a privation that can never be restored or made whole again simply by adding in the missing component.... It is only that new kind of art which reflexively perceives this problem and lives this formal dilemma that can be called modernism in the first place.[15]

Richardson's sprawling, attentive, open-ended novel lives this formal dilemma and has its readers live it too. If it rejects from the outset a contemporary sense of an ending, the nostalgia for a time before the war which was peaceful, stable, and forever England, it is because *Pilgrimage* remembers differently, refusing any simple notion of the modern as a break with a homogeneous and tradition-bound past. This is a narrative that recognizes privation – what has been left out – as a more general predicament: which, as we will see, works through mourning as part of the very structure of modernity itself.

ENCOUNTERING PROUST

> I cut all those 5 vols. piecemeal, leaving them all over the room, and read them the same way, taking up the first handy vol. and opening at random. At last the whole hung and hangs, a tapestry all around me.[16]

The 'magic of the woven text' (iii. 251) that *Pilgrimage* celebrates was not for Dorothy Richardson dependent on the conventional organization of a linear plot or the finality of a storyline. Her novel could be picked up and read arbitrarily from one point to another, she felt, much as in her own reading of five volumes of Proust the improvisation of a 'cut-up' assemblage – long before

William Burroughs – allowed her to create her own *Recherche*.

Proust's novel evidently shares with *Pilgrimage* a central focus on the process of memory itself. As Walter Benjamin observes, in a statement which is equally relevant to Richardson's narrative: 'Only the *actus purus* of recollection itself, not the author or the plot, constitutes the unity of the text. One may even say that the intermittence of author and plot is only the reverse of the continuum of memory, the pattern on the back side of the tapestry.' [17] It is no coincidence that two such epic works should labour 'in search of lost time' at this point, conveying, in Benjamin's terms again, 'an idea of the efforts it took to restore the figure of the storyteller to the present generation'.[18] In both, remembering serves as a form of apprenticeship that will free the protagonist to become a writer. Both narratives are founded on a form of attentiveness in which the fleeting fragments of everyday life yield up an archaeology of memory. As Marcel, Proust's narrator, observes: 'An hour is not merely an hour, it is a vase filled with perfumes, with sounds, with projects, with climates. What we call reality is a relation between those sensations and those memories which simultaneously encircle us.'[19]

In Proust's narrative, however, retrieval of the past ultimately involves the search for a state of timelessness – 'fragments of existence withdrawn from time'. His novel attempts an aesthetic flight from the transitoriness of the present, and from the dead weight of sedimented time, as in the final vision of the post-war matinée where the Guermantes appear in Richardson's words 'tottering alone and aghast upon the summit of the piled-up, unique, incommunicable years' (CBP 161). Although *Pilgrimage* seems occasionally to seek out a similar contemplative condition, whether in the epiphanic intensity of Miriam's memory of childhood bliss, her 'bee-memory', or in the desire for 'the Now, the eternal moment' (iv. 635) expressed in the later volumes, it does not succumb to such an escape. Rather it returns to the present in a more complex way as a shifting constellation of temporalities which deepens and renews itself with age. The past opens on to its future in *Pilgrimage*; the present is a continual performance: 'While I write, everything vanishes but what I contemplate. The whole of what is called "the past" is with me, seen anew, vividly. No, Schiller, the past does not stand "being still". It moves, growing with one's growth.

11

Contemplation is adventure into discovery; reality' (iv. 657).

The difference between the narratives of Proust and Richardson centres on their relation to the historicity that the past represents. Most significantly, Richardson's narrativization of memory as an 'adventure into discovery' in the present takes place in the context of a sustained reflection on the nature of women's experience. In this search for 'lost time', the act of memory is also one of material recuperation, whereby the 'masses left unexpressed' by the dominant culture – the patterns of women's lives, the shape of their desires, their *duration* in history – might be brought into the aesthetic form of the novel.

TECHNOLOGIES OF MEMORY

> A monument does not commemorate or celebrate something that happened but confides to the ear of the future the persistent sensations that embody the event.[20]

The associative drive of Richardson's narrative thus performs what it is seeking out: a quality of experience 'proper' – in the sense of belonging – to women. In formal terms Richardson had developed something quite new, 'for which we still seek a name' as Woolf put it in her review: 'she has invented a sentence we might call a psychological sentence of the feminine gender.'[21] In generic terms her narrative was also difficult to situate. A woman's *Bildungsroman* – a novel of the protagonist's self-development and thus emancipation – *Pilgrimage* resists the seductive comforts of the romance plot which reinforces restrictive models of marriage and familial life, while drawing on the fantasies and desires encoded in such conventions. The narrative pushes a realist premiss – 'the close rendering of ordinary experience' – beyond its limits, the sheer inclusiveness of detail refusing the refuge of story. With its realization that 'the torment of all [male] novels is what is left out' (iv. 239), the novel begins to write a notion of women's experience into the symbolic fictions by which a dominant culture both reproduces and comes to know itself: the struggle with form is a process of coming to terms with the social construction of gender.

Central to this struggle is the nature of cultural memory. The narrative articulates itself through the presentation of specific technologies of memory which are themselves different forms of aesthetic production: architecture, photography, painting, cinematography. These are not present in the text in any systematic sense, operating as much through allusion and fragmentary reference as by some fundamental design, but they are nevertheless one important means of understanding the aesthetic (and political) logic of the novel. It is through these technologies that the narrative 'confides to the ear of the future', in the words of Deleuze and Guattari, the experience of the past as the 'becoming-child of the present'.[22]

Building as Monument

Architecture provides an oblique point of departure. The title of the first volume – *Pointed Roofs* – immediately recalls John Ruskin, for whom the pointed arch was not only the feature most characteristic of gothic architecture but also a major signal of cultural difference: 'I know not any features which make the contrast between continental domestic architecture, and our own, more humiliatingly felt, or which give so sudden a feeling of new life and delight ... as the quaint points and pinnacles of the roof gables.'[23] Richardson's title is thus appropriate enough for a volume which takes its protagonist, educated in a Ruskin-influenced school, on a passage to Europe and the gabled houses of German towns, locating her formation firmly in a nineteenth-century context. Yet it also suggests more.

'Gothic effects bring nostalgia, have a deep recognizable quality of life. A gothic house is a person, a square house is a thing ...', Miriam explains in the later volume of *Oberland* (iv. 25). For Ruskin, at the time when, as he argued in 'The Lamp of Memory', 'the place both of the past and the future is too much usurped in our minds by the restless and discontented present', the architecture of ancient buildings offered a link with past tradition.[24] Buildings presented a form of historical memory, marked by the labour of those who had built them. Theirs was a 'mysterious sympathy' for the alienated inhabitants of a new and devalued age.

In *Pilgrimage* old buildings embody the continuity of this form of Ruskinian memory for Miriam Henderson, suggested in the contemplative air of the 'ancient thick-walled house' (iv. 411) of Dimple Hill, or in the more abstracted grey lines and 'finely-etched streets' (iii. 247) of the London scene, bathed in the golden light Ruskin ascribes to them. True to this conservative romanticism, Miriam often finds in ancient city buildings and pavements her link with nature: London as prairie, as harvest. Conversely, modern housing, particularly that of the suburbs, suggests stark, grim modernist uniformity, its porchlessness signal to the loss of that Ruskinian heritage: 'long rows of houses streamed by, their close ranks broken up by an occasional cross-road. They were large, high flat-fronted houses with flights of grey stone steps leading to porchless doors' (i. 195).

Yet, as I have begun to argue, Miriam Henderson is not in flight from a 'restless and discontented' present, though she experiences the pressures of modernity acutely enough. It is after all from this point in time that the voices of women can newly be heard, cut loose from the traditions that have constrained them. If the allusion to Ruskin allows us to identify one strand of cultural memory at work in *Pilgrimage* – one, moreover, which underlines the romantic anti-capitalism informing the novel – it is a romance with the past which is not wholly indulged: it leaves out as much as it memorializes. Miriam cannot always recognize herself in the historical memory contained within a building: 'the room was old and experienced, full like her inmost mind of the unchanging past. Nothing in her life had any meaning for it' (ii. 334). If architecture here offers the possibility of a memorialization of national culture, in Ruskinian form it suggests a form of Englishness in curious stasis, impassive, unable to recognize itself in the troubling demands of the new.

Photograph as Monument

This sense of dislocation, of a past and a present engaged in a vain search for mutual recognition, is a facet of modern women's experience in *Pilgrimage*. As she thinks back through family history in an attempt to discover her identity there, Miriam's memory is meditated by photographs:

> Whatever might be the truth about heredity, it was immensely disturbing to be pressed upon by two families, to discover, in their so different qualities, the explanation of oneself. The sense of existing merely as a link, without individuality, was not at all compensated by the lifting, and distribution backwards, of responsibility. [...] Boldly faced in the light of her new interest, the vividly remembered forms,

and paintings and photographs almost as vividly real, came forward and grouped themselves about her as if mournfully glad of the long-deferred opportunity. They offered, not themselves, but what they saw and knew. (iii. 247)

Photography, as Rosalind Krauss has argued, 'is an agent in the collective fantasy of family cohesion'; [25] in *Pilgrimage* it functions as a sign of dislocation as much as cohesive confirmation. While here Miriam manages in the light and dark of the remembered photograph to discover truths about her own place in family history, elsewhere photographs appear rather more deceptive, signs of the alienation of modern life, or its kaleidoscopic ephemerality. Eyes often take photographs in *Pilgrimage* as if by way of possession; phrases, fragments of language, are seen to resemble them; experiences are lived as if continuations of them: 'Miriam felt as if they were a bit of the photograph walking up the hill' (i. 312). When women appear caught in the frame the photograph becomes testimony to masquerade: 'she was not a woman, she was a *woman*' (i. 400).

'Never before has an age been so informed about itself, if being informed means having an image of objects that resembles them in a photographic sense,' wrote Siegfried Kracauer in the 1920s. 'But the flood of photos sweeps away the dams of memory ... Never before has a period known so little about itself.'[26] This is a paradox explored in *Pilgrimage*, in which the photograph memorializes the instance where meaning may have been, a sign of historical fatality. More broadly, photography becomes a metaphor for the way modern life is experienced as a series of arrested moments, moments 'without future', in Roland Barthes's words.[27] It becomes possible to read the novel as a woman's *Waste Land* to the extent that it represents contemporary existence as a fragmentary disorder, marked by the traces of the past, the unity of which remains unknown.

Yet, while *Pilgrimage* is touched at times by a kind of conservative melancholy, such a reading is not sustainable. The novel also, importantly, celebrates the energies released by modernity, of which the photograph becomes almost a Promethean symptom. Attending a lecture on the photographic method of Daguerre with her employer, Mr Hancock, Miriam is fascinated: '... waves of light which would rush through the film at enormous speed and get away into space without leaving any

15

impression, were stopped by some special kind of film and when surging up and down in confinement – making strata ...' (ii. 106). The effect of colour photography has an almost epiphanic intensity:

> There was something in this intense hard rich colour like something one sometimes saw when it wasn't there, a sudden brightening and brightening of all colours till you felt something must break if they grew any brighter – or in the dark, or in one's mind, suddenly, at any time, unearthly brilliance. (ii. 107)

Photography here snatches meaning from light, less a memorialization of the past than an articulation of the contingency of change and movement in the present.

Painting: Beyond Monument

The consciousness of Miriam Henderson gradually becomes like the light-sensitive surface of photographic film – a 'delicate and efficient receiving instrument', as Lawrence Hyde called her in the *Adelphi*.[28] The narrative moves on from its Ruskinian beginnings, opening up to the 'uncertainty, noise, speed, movement [and] rapidity of external change' of a 'new mental climate', as Richardson described in *Close Up* (*CU*9 306). This is in part a painful process, involving a letting-go of a past which 'still had the power to lead one back through any small crushing maiming aperture' (ii. 315–16). Miriam, a modernist, learns to forget.

'Coming events cast *light*' (ii. 13), Miriam states. The narrative becomes intensely abstract at certain moments, achieving almost painterly impressionism, which captures both the experience of mobile city life and the pressure to move constantly into the future: 'everything breaking into light just in front of you, making you almost fall off the edge into the expanse coming up before you' (ii. 42). 'Every one, merely by being alive and not sure of the whence and the whither, must be helplessly impressionist' (iii. 493), Miriam explains. As she walks through the West End, the architecture gives way to her perceptual experience:

> THE West End street ... grey buildings rising on either side, angles sharp against the sky ... softened angles of buildings against other buildings ... high moulded angles soft as crumb, with deep undershadows ... creepers fraying from the balconies ... strips of window blossoms across the buildings, scarlet, yellow, high up; a

16

confusion of lavender and white pouching out along the dipping sill
... a wash of green creeper up a white painted house-front ... patches
of shadow and bright light ... Sounds of visible near things streaked
and scored with broken light as they moved, led off into distant
sounds ... chiming together. (ii. 416)

Colours, shapes, spaces: the narrative of *Pilgrimage* employs
sensory abstraction and ellipsis to convey the 'new and nameless
experience' that Roger Fry saw as the role of the work of art.[29]
Such an art was possible only through the rejection of the burden
of memory, of tradition, he argued. Describing Roger Fry
rendered speechless before a late Cézanne landscape, via the
account of a witness, Virginia Woolf, Rosalind Krauss concludes:

what he saw there was a pattern, he was to explain, a pattern forged by
the creative 'look' that artists possess as they scan the chaotic rubble of
ordinary appearances and, through an extraordinary act of selective
seeing, manage to extract a series of intervals, of harmonic relation-
ships between darks and lights, an intuition of that organic
intermeshing to which could be affixed the term *unity*. What this
look entails is, at one and the same time, utter detachment from the
objects themselves – their meaning, their worth, their moral value (so
much for Mr Ruskin!) – and complete passion about the implications
of form.[30]

Yet the Bloomsburian modernist credos of impersonality and
significant form sit uneasily with Richardson's work, which, as
Woolf was to complain, lacked a fundamental unity, and seemed,
despite its evident experimentalism, muddled about the 'implications of form'. On the one hand, such impressionism is not enough
in *Pilgrimage*, which seeks to found its aesthetic on a form even
more mobile than the creative 'look'. On the other, 'detachment'
seems a complex issue in a text which is about the cost of
impersonality for the woman writer, in experiential and artistic
terms.[31] One of the reasons that Richardson's work disappeared
from view, even though the *Sphere* newspaper reported in 1924 that
she was 'reputed to have influenced more writers than any other
English woman writer of today',[32] may have been this lack of 'fit'
with what has become a dominant ideology of modernism. Taking
such an ideology as her aesthetic standard, her biographer Gloria
Fromm suggested that Richardson had chosen 'life' over the
'classical calm' of a Joyce or Woolf.[33] Here was the source of her
failure. Richardson's aesthetic 'choice' needs to be read in a more

complex light as a challenge to that ideology.

Film: Memorializing the Modern

> The cinema has become so much a habit of thought and word and deed as to make it impossible to visualise modern consciousness without it.[34]

So Kenneth Macpherson wrote in 1928 as editor of *Close Up*, 'the only magazine devoted to the film as an art'. Dorothy Richardson, a regular contributor and film-goer from at least 1921, would have concurred. 'More than any other single factor,' she wrote, 'cinema has contributed to the change in the mental climate' (*CU*9 306). If *Pilgrimage* is a narrative in search of an aesthetic form, then the moving image of silent cinema finally provided it.

'The memories accumulated since she landed were like a transparent film through which clearly she saw all she had left behind; and felt the spirit of it waiting within her to project itself upon things just ahead' (iv. 141). It is the language of cinematography that shapes the subjective landscape of *Pilgrimage* (as it does the psychoanalytical topography of Freud): its dynamism, its complex temporality. Insistently, the metaphor of the 'screen' marks a patterning of repression in the text, of masking and projection. It also provides a means of staging the complex nature of cultural memory within modernity, as will become clear.

Cinematography underlines that the modern 'stream of consciousness', a 'moving vista' continually invoked within *Pilgrimage* seemingly as a private, individualized vision of the world, was in fact collectively shared, a 'common possession of all who would be still' (iii. 114). And Richardson knew it. If the modern world is life 'speeded up', as Hypo Wilson suggests (whose name Richardson derived from the 'Acid Hypo' used to fix film), for 'today we are on the move, we've got to be on the move, or things will run away with us' (iv. 334), it is the technology of film which captures such an experience, and provides a place from which to view it. And in the urban picture – places which Richardson visited, it was overwhelmingly an experience embraced by women. 'School, salon, brothel, bethel, newspaper, art, science, religion, philosophy, commerce, sport and adventure; flashes of beauty of all sorts. The only anything and everything,' Richardson enthused. 'And here we all are, as never before. What will it do with us?' (*CU2* 65). To find out, and to discover how it shaped her aesthetic challenge, we have to take a number of routes through *Pilgrimage* itself.

2

Screen Memories

Proust could appear as a phenomenon only in a generation that had lost all bodily, natural expediences for remembering, and, poorer than before, was left to its own devices, and thus could only get hold of the children's world in an isolated, scattered, and pathological fashion.

Walter Benjamin

In 1924 Ernest Hemingway published Dorothy Richardson's 'The Garden' in *Transatlantic Review*. In this short story she draws on material associated with her own earliest bee-memory, to dramatize the event of a small child first discovering herself through her relation with the natural world. It is a story about the beginnings of consciousness. A later autobiographical sketch underlines its resonance for Richardson: 'Berkshire was also a vast garden, flowers, bees and sunlight, a three-in-one, at once enchantment and a benevolent conspiracy of awareness turned towards a small being to whom they first, and they alone, brought the sense of existing' (B. 110–11). There is an air of mysticism about this Edenic founding of selfhood in a Berkshire garden, where the child moves in a magical sphere presided over by a natural and sentient trinity of flowers, bees, and sunlight. It is a scene that connotes innocence, security, and, above all, *home*, for Richardson, the lost garden of her Babington childhood. And it surfaces, reinscribed in fragments and allusions, within the narrative of Miriam Henderson, as the moment 'when the strange independent joy had begun' (i. 316). As such, it is presented as a founding event, and one that deserves our attention – a place from which to begin to trace the anatomy of memory at work in *Pilgrimage* in more detail.

'The Garden' is the fullest narrativization of the scene that serves in Richardson's work, then, as a form of ur-memory. Like the first

20

pages of Joyce's *Portrait*, though without the controlling parental free indirect discourse, it leads the reader directly into a child's consciousness. This child's thought with its precise, syntactical flow and repetition, has an almost Steinian simplicity. As she ventures down the gravel path, the child attempts to measure herself in and through the world of sensations that surrounds her. Richardson uses synaesthesia, one sense evoked in terms of another, to represent the child's dissolving of the boundaries between her own experience and the garden, between subject and object. Smells are visible: 'She could see the different smells going up into the sunshine. The sunshine smelt of the flowers' (G. 21). Inanimate objects are endowed with feelings: paths 'ache with going so fast' (G. 23); bees talk 'about the different colours coming out at the tops of the stalks' (G. 21); flowers offer up their affection – 'they quickly said they loved her and were nice' – or resemble people: 'it was Nelly on a stalk' (G. 22).

If this event seems to represent an ideal, epiphanic moment for Richardson, it would seem to be because the child's consciousness discovers itself in a rapturous and animistic compact with the natural world. It is an experience Miriam Henderson seeks out in the more dissociated world of *Pilgrimage*: 'Did anybody know this strange thing? She almost ran; *my* "commons," she said. "I only know how beautiful you are; if only I knew whether you know that I know"' (i. 394). Mrs Ramsay, in Woolf's *To the Lighthouse*, reflects on a similar tendency: 'It was odd, she thought, how if one was alone, one leant to things, inanimate things; trees, streams, flowers; felt they expressed one; felt they became one; felt they knew one, in a sense were one; felt an irrational tenderness thus ... as for oneself.'[2]

Suzanne Raitt has usefully discussed such a blurring of subject–object boundaries in experimental fiction of the period in the context of the cultural 'pull of mysticism' at the time, and of the popularity of the Bergson of *Creative Evolution* with his concept of intuitive perception as a form of flowing intellection. For May Sinclair in 1917, who first ascribed the term 'stream of consciousness' to Richardson's narrative in the following year, mysticism was undergoing a 'serious revival'.[3] As Raitt argues in *Vita and Virginia*, it offered women a particular means of representing selfhood:

In much women's autobiography, mysticism is seen as the beginning of the whole problem, the engendering of subjectivity itself. Women's autobiographical self-construction often takes as its point of departure a moment of almost extra-corporeal intensity – Dorothy Richardson's 'bee-memory' in *Pilgrimage*, for example. A mystical experience is located as the initiation of a sense of identity, the origin to which subsequent events are always accountable.[4]

There is no doubt that *Pilgrimage* presents moments of experiential intensity in precisely this sense: 'Why was the spring suddenly so real? Why was it that you could stand as it were in a shaft of it all the time, feeling in your breathing, hearing in your voice the sound of the spring, the blood in your fingertips seeming like the roses that they would touch soon in the garden?' (i. 392). The anticipatory form of this reverie does seem Bergsonian in its subjunctive absorption of the subject. While Richardson later denied the specific influence of his work, she acknowledged that he 'was putting into words something then dawning within the human consciousness.'[5] We are yet to discover, though, how such moments are inflected within her narrative.

In any event 'The Garden' does not quite deliver its epiphany in this mystical form. It is as if by narrating it the short story is also offering a reading of the experience, reworking it. Indeed what seems Edenic about the scene is less its image of natural communion, which is clearly informed by a child's egocentric sense of a world that exists only for her gaze, than the possibility of loss, as we will see. If there is a moment of 'enchantment' here, however, it is a distinctly unBergsonian one. Where Bergson, as Raitt points out, understands consciousness (and representation) as incompatible with action, since it is 'produced when the mind goes ahead of, or exceeds the body',[6] what is striking about the representation of a child's consciousness in Richardson's story is its direct connection of perception and action. Body and consciousness are here indivisible; knowledge is tactile, a creative form of improvisation: a mimetic mastery of the world. It is in this active, material sense, then, rather than in any ineffable grounding of subjectivity, that the child can be seen here, in the words of Walter Benjamin, as 'representative of Paradise'.[7] 'The Garden', however, tests this founding moment further.

THE GARDEN-SCREEN

In her biography of Richardson, Gloria Fromm was surely right to detect the influence of the film medium on 'The Garden', in its 'photographic' registering of a 'moving picture of consciousness'.[8] The story moves along by a series of close-ups and long shots, governed by the child's actions and fluctuating mood, opening with an interaction of movement, space, and sound that is almost stroboscopically arrested: 'There was no one there. The sound of feet and no one there. The gravel stopped making its noise when she stood still. When the last foot came down all the flowers stood still.' (G. 21). At the end of the story, when the child tumbles down abruptly, the details are given as if in slow motion:

> Bang. The hard gravel holding a pain against her nose. Someone calling. She lay still hoping her nose would be bleeding to make them sorry. Here was crying again. Coming up out of body, into her face, hot, twisting it up, lifting it away from the gravel to let out the noise. (G. 23–4)

For Walter Benjamin the new technologies of camera and film promised to restore to human consciousness, distracted and traumatized by the shocks of modern existence, the perceptual capacity he valued in children's cognition. 'With the close-up, space expands; with slow motion, movement is extended. The enlargement of a snapshot does not simply render more precise what in any case was visible, though unclear: it reveals entirely new structural formations of the subject.'[9] Bodily gesture, expression, and the most habitual of actions could, under the eye of the camera, suddenly be perceived anew. Film, he argued, had revealed 'an immense and unexpected field of action', an 'optical unconscious': 'it becomes clear that a different nature speaks to the camera than to the naked eye – different above all in this, that in place of space interwoven with the consciousness of human beings, one is presented with a space unconsciously interwoven.'[10]

Through its representation of infant perception, 'The Garden' allows the reader access to this realm of 'different nature', one permeated by bodily sensation, spontaneous fantasy, and unconscious desires. What is more, Richardson's narrative subjects the child's experience to a form of filmic – optical –

23

testing. It is not just that the child's play reveals her deep anxiety at the unknown outside world where 'it is dark and cold' (G. 23) – suggested by the reassuring anthropomorphism of the flowers that 'put their arms around her' (G. 21), which know 'about the other part of the garden' (G. 22) and may protect her from the 'It' that lurks 'far away down the path where it was different' (G. 23). More significantly, in its breaking-up of the action of the child into a sequence of arrested moments of sensation and motion, the narrative offers us the slow-motion mechanics of another psychic drama: one centring on parental loss.

In *Beyond the Pleasure Principle* Sigmund Freud described the way a small boy had turned the experience of his mother's absence into a game, by staging the disappearance and return of a wooden reel. This 'good little boy' allows his mother to leave without yelling his protest, having compensated himself through play by mimicking and thereby gaining mastery over what was distressing him. Indeed Freud reads a form of defiance into the child's hurling away of the toy: 'All right, then, go away! I don't need you. I'm sending you away myself.'[11] The child represented in 'The Garden', who also seeks out confirmation that she is 'happy and good', plays a game which we might interpret in the light of Freud's example. She also makes things appear there and not-there, uniquely able, she tells herself, to see how the flowers go 'on being how they were when no one was there ... *They* had never seen them like this' (G. 21). Flowers seem 'not so nice' and then 'quickly say they love her'; threaten to go away and then 'kiss her gently' (G. 22); make the garden safe but refuse to follow her. As she runs back to the security of the house, projecting her feelings on to the 'frightened' plants, she falls down, registering pain. She hears 'someone calling' – the mother's voice? – and wants to punish them, 'make them sorry' (G. 23). And she expects a tribute to mark her success. 'The flowers were unkind, staying too far off to tell them how happy and good she was.' (G. 24).

What does it mean to read the story in this way? What began as an event representing communion with nature – in Richardson's autobiographical sketch denoting the almost mystical emergence of subjectivity – is revealed as a different kind of drama, a child's acting-out of her mother's absence/loss, of her anxiety at independence. Her consciousness not only parries the sensations that excite her from outside, it also shields her from unconscious fears through projection and mimicry. If Richardson's bee-memory is presented as a founding event within her work, then, as Freud puts it in the same essay, it may be a 'memory-trace' which 'has nothing to do with the fact of becoming conscious', but which is 'most powerful and most enduring when the process which left [it] behind was one which never entered consciousness'.[12]

The psychic structure of memory is articulated in Freud's work in metaphors taken from different visual technologies – from the photographic apparatus to the screening of moving pictures. All childhood memories, he argued, are 'plastically visual', and 'whether in fact they prove to be true or falsified, what one sees invariably includes oneself as a child, with a child's shape and clothes'. Moreover, he suspected:

> that in the so-called earliest childhood memories we possess not the genuine memory-trace but a later revision of it, a revision which may have been subjected to the influences of a variety of later psychical forces. Thus the 'childhood memories' of individuals come in general to acquire the significance of 'screen memories'.[13]

Richardson's earliest memory, that claimed by Miriam Henderson in *Pilgrimage* as the moment when 'the strange independent joy had begun', can be read as a screen memory; 'The Garden' another revision, or screening, of it. The intense bee-memory may serve to represent a transcendent moment in Richardson's work, but its material has been reworked, in time, a labour the narrative of *Pilgrimage* takes as its object.

THE LOST GARDEN

> The present can be judged by the part of the past it brings up. If the present brings up the happiness of the past, the present is happy. [...] If you are happy in the present something is being expiated. (ii. 402)

Such is the repetition and density of information contained in the narrative of *Pilgrimage* that the focus on the recurrence of a single topos may appear almost arbitrary: so much is invested in each fraction of every event, in the 'systole and diastole' of Richardson's text. For some readers the diet proved too much – D. H. Lawrence, in 1923, among them: 'It is self-consciousness picked into such fine bits that the bits are most of them invisible, and you have to go by smell. Through thousands and thousands of pages Mr Joyce and Miss Richardson tear themselves to pieces, strip their emotions to the finest threads...'[14]

Yet this is a novel that in one sense demands its own piecemeal consumption, refusing us a neat or even ironic refuge in any overarching overview, plan, or mythic key. It is a narrative that, for all its flowing momentum, deals in fragments. In thinking through his own approach to Proust's *Remembrance of Things Past*, Theodor Adorno characterizes Proustian narrative in a way which is equally relevant to *Pilgrimage*. Here, too, is a text that 'crystallizes out of intertwined individual presentations. Each of them conceals within itself constellations of what ultimately emerges as the idea of the novel... The *durée* the work investigates is concentrated in countless moments, often isolated from one another.'[15]

In tracing the recurrence of one such moment in the 'rank vegetal proliferation', as Adorno put it, of this narrative, we are provided with a way in. Moreover, Richardson's bee-memory presents itself as a beginning – the mark of a child's first experience of independence, in a novel about a woman's search for autonomy. As such, it is charged with significance. We begin, then, with fragments.

The Babington garden surfaces on a number of occasions in the early volumes of *Pilgrimage*. Triggered in two instances by a visit to the seaside – the landscape of childhood holidays and of her seaside villa home – Miriam Henderson's 'first memory' comes powerfully to mind through her senses: the moment

> when she had found herself toddling alone along the garden path between beds of flowers almost on a level with her head and blazing in the sunlight. [...] She could see the flowers distinctly as she walked quickly back through the esplanade; they were sweet williams and 'everlasting' flowers, the sweet williams smelling very strongly sweet in her nostrils, and one shiny brown everlasting flower that she had touched with her nose, smelling like hot paper. (i. 317)

Each time the scene carries the same connotations for Miriam: independence and freedom, a moment when she had found herself 'outside life, untouched by anything'; acute happiness in a timeless world, 'no winters, no times of day or changes to be seen'; a moment innocently unaware of 'any end to being in the bright sun' (ii. 213), and thus marked in its present incarnation by the eventuality of loss. As Miriam remarks to her companion in *Deadlock*, 'I often dream I am there [...] and I feel then as if going away were still to come, an awful thing that had never happened' (iii. 124).

At each point in the narrative, however, Miriam's recollection of the garden serves a different purpose, indicating the facets and limits of her development, embedded in a kind of density of subjective action. It is introduced in a constellation of reference, shadowed and refigured by other events, other memories. If we read this account of Miriam's earliest memory, as Freud suggested, as a screen memory, then it both conceals and – through disavowal – calls attention to a site of psychic pain. And that pain, indeed, may post-date the image that screens it. Screen memories, Freud suggested, can have a number of different temporal relations to the experience they replace. While their content may belong to the earliest years of childhood, they may substitute, retroactively, for mental experiences that occurred later in life. The narrative thus presents us with a complex tissue of psychic and temporal relations, though Miriam is, through her screen memory, keeping it at bay.

THREE INSTANCES

Independence, then, yet loneliness. In *Backwater* Miriam has to search out, 'try to remember', the origin for her 'strange independent joy'. Sitting on the beach alone, in Mrs Ramsay's words, she 'leans' to her environment: 'her mind slid out making a strange half-familiar compact with all these things. She was theirs, she would remember them all, always. They were not alone, because she was with them and knew them.' Miriam remembers an earlier confirmation of this same compact in a childhood 'unpermitted wandering' over the cliffs, when she had gone home delighted with this secret communion, which had made her forget a 'strange lady' on the jetty 'who had caught her in her arms and horribly kissed her'. The link between sexuality and Miriam's secret is obliquely made here; the significance of this memory, however, centrally involves her relationship with her mother. Miriam cannot share her secret: 'when they questioned her, it seemed that there was only the lady to tell them about.' And now, in the narrative present, 'it would hardly ever come; there were always people talking' (i. 316).

27

At this point, then, Miriam recalls the Babington garden as the origin of her secret joy, one she is unable to communicate. 'It would be impossible to speak to any one about them unless one felt perfectly sure that the other person felt about them in the same way and knew that they were more real than anything else in the world.' As if by a kind of photo-imposition, Miriam's thoughts about the present here shadow her childhood experience: the strange kiss, here from Miss Meldrum of the boarding house, which 'made her feel as if there were some sly secret between them' (i. 317); her inability to make her mother understand this inner happiness, both in the past – 'it's your splendid health – and the influence of the Holy Spirit' (i. 318) – and in the present, when 'with the operation and all the uncertainty ahead she would probably cry' (i. 317).

'Useless to try to talk about anything.... Mother would be somehow violent. She would be overpowering' (i. 195), Miriam observes earlier in *Backwater*. Her bee-memory is inevitably connected in this second volume of *Pilgrimage* with her mother, and the adolescent pain of independence and loss. Here Miriam can only access the experience represented by the Babington garden when alone, and then through voluntary memory, blocked from her secret by 'the weary round of words' that stands for everyday life. Her secret 'would fade more and more'. 'What was life? Either playing a part all the time in order to be amongst people in the warm, or standing alone with the strange true real feeling – alone with a sort of edge of reality on everything' (i. 320).

On its next appearance the Babington garden forms part of a meditation on the nature of memory itself. Its recurrence in *The Tunnel* parallels and comments on the earlier occasion. Miriam is visiting the coast, this time with her girl friends Mag and Jan rather than with her family, and happier in their company than being alone. It is nevertheless in the seclusion of half-sleepy reverie that she sees 'perfect things all round her, no beginning or ending':

> She had thought they belonged to the past, to childhood and youth. In childhood she had thought each time that the world had just begun and would always be like that; later on, she remembered, she had always thought when such a moment came that it would be the last, and had clung to it with wide desperate staring eyes until tears came

and she had turned away from some great open scene, with a strong conscious body flooded suddenly by a strong warm tide, to the sad dark world to live for the rest of her time upon a memory. But the moment she had just lived was the same, it was exactly the same as the first one she could remember, the moment of standing, alone, in bright sunlight on a narrow gravel path in the garden at Babington between two banks of flowers [...] (ii.213)

Miriam's earliest memory is restored to her as 'the same' as her present moment, by the very fact of its being 'outside life'. It is lifted out of time, its connectives cut with the Babington garden as an experienced event, as Miriam reflects: 'Yet she must somehow have got out of the house and through the shrubbery and along the plain path between the lawns' (ii. 213). Despite her earlier despair at its 'fading', this sensual merging with the world, an 'oceanic feeling' in Freud's terms is seemingly still available to her, represented as a repetition of the eternal in the present.[16] What distinguishes her bee-memory here from the other sensuous fragments recalled from the past is its involuntary quality, the fact that it comes 'without thought or effort'. The other 'whole pieces of life' come 'up bit by bit as one thought', but are, in contrast, 'all mixed with sadness and pain and bothers with people'.

'*Memory*', Miriam concludes, 'was happiness'. The Babington garden is, like the memorialization of her time in Germany – both moments of the 'strange independent joy' – a place of refuge from 'everything in the difficult life' (ii. 214). It is a screen marked by the projections of an almost desperate will to happiness, which are intensified even more by denial: 'As long as I can sometimes feel like this nothing has mattered. Life is a chain of happy moments that cannot die' (ii. 215). Independence, then, and loss. And, in the vision of the 'happy confidence of the open scene', which is both Germany and Berkshire, homesickness.

Gradually the pavements and 'green spaces' of London become Miriam's home. With this shift, the bee-memory takes on, chameleon-like, new colours – the independence which it marks increasingly accessible. Moving 'along a pathway that led backwards towards a single memory' (iii. 197), Miriam discovers it to be a 'path of advance' into the future. With this experience comes recognition. Where in the past the secret has been impossible to share, now she sees its mark on the faces of other women:

She felt, turned upon her, the welcoming, approving eyes of women she had contemptuously neglected, and upon her own face the dawning reflection of their wise, so irritating smile. She recognized them, half fearfully, for they alone were the company gathered about her as she watched the opening marvel. She recognized them for lonely wanderers upon the earth. They, these women, were the only people who *knew*. Their smile was the smile of these wide vistas, wrought and shaped, held back by the pity they turned towards the blind life of men; but it was *alone* in its vision of the spaces opening beyond the world of daily life. (iii. 197–8)

If the bee-memory screens, in some sense, the cost (and necessity) of the loss of the mother for the newly independent modern woman, it also becomes the means of envisaging a dispersed collectivity of women, all initiates into the 'secret'. Miriam, pursuing this path, 'must be always alone'; but she is 'supported' in the humdrum world of the everyday by the 'signs and smiles' of other equally lonely women on the same journey. 'There is a moment in meeting a woman, any woman, the first moment, before speech, when everything becomes new; the utter astonishment of life is there, speech seems superfluous, even with women who have not consciously realized that life is astonishing,' Miriam muses in *Revolving Lights* (iii. 280). It is this experience of the 'new' that *Pilgrimage* attempts to represent, in which women become the custodians of modernity.

In connecting these fragments, the barest of profiles, of narrative movements, is sketched out. A passage from the country to the city, between the past and the present. A story about experience, and the difficulty of communication, the obstructiveness of language. A presentation of different facets of loss – of home, of the mother, of the past – and the restorative powers of memory. And throughout, a curious *pas de deux* between the intensities of a subjective life and the unsatisfying demands of the everyday – the latter serving as both an intransigent block and yet banal route to this 'true real feeling'. Yet the bee-memory also holds within itself a phantasmatic possibility of recuperation, in which a community of experience between women can be imagined. Before we can explore this experience, the narrative's representation of 'loss' has to be understood.

However much Miriam wants to share this inaugural moment

with others, it remains a solitary one in the early volumes of *Pilgrimage*. As soon as it enters the world of 'talk', the bee-memory, like other childhood recollections, loses its magic. It is not only Michael Shatov of *Deadlock* whose attention wanders as Miriam recounts her memories, but other listeners, other readers. Like the reader of Proust, who saw boredom as an integral part of the fascination of the *Recherche*, since 'all ordinary dreams turn into pointless stories as soon as one tells them to someone',[17] the reader of Richardson has in part to contend with the banality of someone else's dreams. In *Pilgrimage* Miriam has to negotiate this fact as a kind of Fall, voicing memories 'so sacred and so secret' that she wishes she had never mentioned them, 'pressing alone wearily on through the dying interest of the hearers' (ii. 299). Moreover, as soon as such memories are embedded in narrative, they threaten to betray that which they screen: repeatedly, a story of loss.

THE LOSS-SCREEN

The bee-memory thus figures as a leave-taking, the loss of home, even as it will eventually hold out, in the London landscape, the potentiality of return. *Pilgrimage* itself, as *Bildungsroman*, stages and re-stages the event of leave-taking in different forms – caught up irrevocably in the parental loss that we saw acted out in 'The Garden'. If we remember Freud's definition of the earliest memory as a screen memory, one which can substitute retro-actively for painful psychic material – that is, though its content might derive from infancy, it screens experience occurring later in life – then we are given a means of thinking the structure of the narrative. What is presented as a formative event in Miriam's self-realization in fact stands in for something more complex in temporal terms. And we are led not simply further into the subjective realism of her 'damned egotistical self', which was Virginia Woolf's complaint about the novel, but into a hidden material history of a woman's life. This childhood memory has a specific pathos in the narrative not simply because of Miriam's own private struggle, but in a more representative, historical sense: it marks a woman's voyage out from the secure home of Victorian tradition into the shock of independent twentieth-century life. In the remaining part of this chapter I will begin to chart this passage.

From the very opening pages of *Pointed Roofs* Miriam is preparing to leave her home. The event that has prompted this move involves loss in a literal sense: her father's bankruptcy, and a subsequent family crisis that has been a long time in the making. The secure world represented by the Babington childhood, one of genteel affluence, is doubly shaken: by the money troubles that will eventually force Miriam to find her way in the working world, and by the illness of her mother, which will end in her suicide. As she leaves for her first teaching job in Germany at the age of 17, Miriam feels relief:

> 'Isn't it ghastly – for all of us?' Miriam felt treacherously outspoken. It was a relief to be going away. She knew that this sense of relief made her able to speak. 'It's never knowing that's so awful. Perhaps he'll get some more money presently and things'll go on again. Fancy mother having it always ever since we were babies.' (i. 18)

Miriam's new awareness of the long-term existence of her mother's illness and the financial crisis allows her to refashion the past. In Germany she now remembers 'her mother's illness, money troubles – their two years at the sea to retrieve ... the disappearance of the sunlit red-walled garden always in full summer sunshine with the sound of bees in it' (i. 32). The bee-memory is thus caught up in this sense of parental crisis.

If this double loss is always intertwined in Miriam's thoughts, as will be seen shortly, her relationship with her father and his failure is more overtly documented in the text. The reverberations of his bankruptcy appear almost traumatic. On the one hand, Miriam will not betray her father and his dreams in public. 'No one else's father' has his taste (i. 33). She is 'at one with him' in his pretence on the train to Germany that she is on the way to finishing school:

> There could be no doubt that he was playing the role of the English gentleman. Poor dear. It was what he had always wanted to be. He had sacrificed everything to the idea of being a 'person of leisure and cultivation'. Well, after all, it was true in a way. He was – and he had, she knew, always wanted her to be the same. (i. 28)

On the other hand, the shame of their loss of class status, and the poverty which makes her 'sick with anxiety' (ii. 116), prove privately corrosive. Far from being a haven, Miriam's family life is

dark and 'pain-shadowed', something to escape, 'driven [...]
again and again to go away and away, anywhere' (ii. 326). In
Backwater, which charts her unhappy months as a North London
teacher, Miriam's depression, and anger, are palpable. *'Honour*
thy father and thy mother. How horribly the words would echo
through the great cold church. *Why* honour thy father and thy
mother? What had they done that was so honourable? Everybody
was dying in cold secret fear. Christ, the son of God, was part of it
all, the same family... vindictive' (i. 255). Like her sisters, 'fellow-
prisoners', Miriam has been 'scored and scarred', bearing the
imprint of 'terrors and uncertainties'. And, even if they have the
power to remake themselves, 'to become quite new', they remain
marked. 'Those American girls in *Little Women* and *Good Wives*
made fun out of everything. But they never had to face real
horrors and hide them from everybody; mewed up' (i. 303).

Miriam, of course, does face real horrors, though in the novel's
chronology of events they have not yet fully unravelled. There is a
curious displacement here, perhaps inevitable in the strange
impossibility of autobiographical writing, in the nature of its
anamnesis: the 'not yet' has always already happened. We might
wish to ascribe her horror to an acute class embarrassment, even
deprivation; there is no doubt that her father's debt is felt as
'disgrace', even as a 'stigma'. Yet the blackness of its effect seems
to stem from elsewhere. The themes of death, illness, and
depression that permeate the world of *Backwater* appear to work
ın anticipation. Miriam shortly learns of her mother's need for an
operation, and, significantly, in shock, 'the garden did not seem to
be there. The tepid night air was like a wall, a black wall' (i. 304).

At the end of the next volume, *Honeycomb*, Miriam discovers, as
Richardson had done, the body of her mother after her suicide –
Richardson's mother had committed suicide by cutting her own
throat. We are given no details of this event, which happens in a
Jamesian form outside the frame of the narrative, between the
paragraphs, though its shock waves are dispersed throughout the
text. It is precisely because of her father's failure that Miriam is
forced to witness this sight: she has been caring for her mother
alone at the seaside as there is no money to provide a nurse. The
loss of the mother, and the daughter's facing of its horror, are thus
entangled with the failure of the father; their new poverty, with
illness and death.

The memory of the Babington garden screens this texture of loss retroactively. But it is also criss-crossed with its traces. Surfacing, as we saw, on Miriam's visits to the seaside – the stage of her mother's death, the destination of her childhood leaving, where she first dreamed of the death of her parents – her bee-memory offers plenitude and timelessness in the place of loss. Her screen memory marks, as we know, a feeling of 'strange independent joy', motivated by a powerful will to happiness. Miriam's vain attempt to share this experience with her mother, since 'there was something true and real somewhere. Mother knew it,' points to a complex knot of identifications which will form the warp and weft of her identity in *Pilgrimage*, hinting at the psychic cost of her voyage out.

Miriam, the third daughter who should have been a son, is the only one who understands, her mother tells her. At times Miriam sees herself as her mother's 'husband. Why have I not been with you all your life?' (i. 456), or, as she explains in *Deadlock*, her mother's son, 'who will give her the understanding she never had from their father' (iii. 220). Miriam's masculine identification positions her as protector, her father's rival; thus, as Jean Radford has argued in a psychoanalytic reading of Miriam's predicament, 'she may even become what her mother desires (and lacks)'.[18] But her masculinity is itself a form of protection, the 'manhood' that shields her from her mother's 'madness', from the maternal voice, elsewhere so comforting, which wants 'to scream, to bellow' (i. 471). Moreover, as that which aligns her with her father, and thus in some sense to blame for her mother's suicide, masculinity is also something to be denied, as Radford points out.

Of interest here is the relation of Miriam's dilemma to the moment of independence signalled by the bee-memory, which is indeed screening a knot of contradiction. If Miriam does at times take her mother's part, acknowledging that 'there was something she had always wanted for herself ... even mother ...' (i. 472), her own autonomy nevertheless depends on breaking away from that maternal tie and all that it represents in the late-Victorian world. In Oedipal terms this is, of course, necessarily the case, but it is rendered most acutely in *Pilgrimage*, where it is ironically her father's failure that propels Miriam out of the home into a painful freedom. If she is critical of him on her mother's behalf, resisting his right to lay down the law, registering the consequences of his

34

failure on her mother's agonized face, she is also in collusion with his class fantasy of improvement and learning. And if marriage might in the future prove her way out of the ignominy of his debt, Miriam has been forewarned – frustrated with the limitations placed on women within married life, of which her mother is a hysterical and rather fearful symptom. Miriam must then also reject her mother, who has the worst of all worlds. She is a failed angel of the house, who has seen through the façade and is punished for her weakness, 'almost killed by things she could not control, having done her duty all her life … doing thing after thing had not satisfied her' (i. 472). And the suppressed violence and anger often attributed to her are clearly Miriam's own. As she discovers in Germany: 'it filled her with fury to be regarded as one of a world of little tame things to be summoned by little man [sic] to be well-willed wives' (i. 129).

The price of Miriam's independence, then, is expressed in the formation of her gendered identity: 'something between a man and a woman, looking both ways' (ii. 187), a 'battlefield of her two natures' (iii. 250). Jean Radford is right to argue that Miriam's guilt at her mother's death is 'textually established *before* the suicide of Mrs Henderson is narrated', that Miriam has in some sense – and not only in Oedipal terms – wished for her mother's death.[19] 'She was a murderess. This was the hidden truth of her life' (iii. 75). Perhaps more subtly, it is also possible to argue that the child Miriam has experienced her mother's evident depression and illness *as* a form of death. [20] Miriam, in any case, rejects her mother's lesson of feminine endurance. 'I'm something new – a kind of different world' (i. 260). The memory of the Babington garden thus substitutes for a constellation of psychic relations, a refuge from a terrain of loss 'unconsciously interwoven' with Miriam's own desires.

A GARDEN INTERIOR

> The garden is a rug onto which the whole world comes to enact its symbolic perfection, and the rug is a sort of garden that can move across space.[21]

By focusing so intently on the subjective dimensions of Miriam Henderson's development, both the novel, and my reading of it, might appear to risk losing sight of wider historical, contextual concerns. Yet the novel does not shy away from what Woolf regarded as 'excrescences of history and fact'.[22] It is precisely in the representation of a young woman's subjectivity that Richardson's narrative reveals the imprint and shadowing of social life, as if in a photographic negative. Indeed it tests it. *Pilgrimage* charts the gap noted by Raymond Williams in the fiction of H. G. Wells, that between 'the pace of history and the pace of a life'.[23] The novel's challenge, to itself and the reader, is to recover that gap; to read 'underneath the surface', as Winifred Bryher described in her review of *Dawn's Left Hand* in 1931, 'the best history yet written of the slow progression from the Victorian period to the modern age'.[24]

In 'The Garden' the child copes with her new-found and tentative freedom by forging a relationship with the natural world around her. Her play allows her to act out her fears. Yet, as I argued earlier, it also represents a particular, mimetic form of cognition, one in which perception, action, and knowledge are indivisible. Miriam Henderson, too, seeks out a feeling of 'compact' with her environment, investing her surroundings with sentience. It is a world she believes is answering her back, returning her gaze, an intersubjective community: 'perhaps, in the end, things, like beloved backgrounds, are people.' Through the action of involuntary memory the most trivial and transient of objects becomes the means of entry into a different space:

> In things, even in perfectly 'ordinary and commonplace things', life is embodied. The sudden sight of a sun-faded garment can arouse from where they lie stored in oneself, sleeping memories, the lovely essences of a summer holiday, free from all that at the moment seemed to come between oneself and the possibility of passionate apprehension. After an interval, only after an interval – showing that there is within oneself something that ceaselessly contemplates 'forgotten' things – a fragment of stone, even a photograph, has the power of making one enter a kingdom one hardly knew one possessed. (iv. 368)

This is the Miriam of *Clear Horizon*, more conceptually aware, more experienced. Yet the unending contemplation of 'forgotten' things which she describes marks her from the early days of the first volumes, set in the 1890s, which have been our focus thus far. And the 'kingdom' offered her by the world of things reveals itself not simply in terms of personal memory, but also as knowledge of a past collective history, a mystery hidden in the everyday world. It signals to her a world she is trying to apprehend even as she is imperceptibly leaving it behind.

Miriam comes upon this mystery in the heart of the domestic interior: the Victorian drawing-room. Going to tea with the Brooms, she describes the furniture in minute, sensuous detail, noting the 'cracked oil-painting of Shakespeare' and 'the new picture of Queen Victoria leaning on a stick and supported by Hindu servants'. The last days of the era. The faces of her hosts are 'heavy, carven, unmoved, age-long', indistinguishable from their surroundings. The furniture is 'silent; beautifully kept' and above all 'experienced': the world it communicates speaks of empire, patriotism, English tradition and disdain for 'the working classes' (i. 343). Seeing the scene through the eyes of her Irish friend, Julia, Miriam refuses to find a place for herself within it.

In the drawing-room of Mrs Bailey's boarding house Miriam undergoes a similar experience. However, the room is here a space of surprises. Unlike the stultifying atmosphere of the Brooms', it contains shocks. The furniture 'seemed to be waiting for someone or something'; a jug's mirrored reflection appears 'extraordinary. Where had it come from? It was an imitation of something. A reflection of some other life. Had it ever been seen by anybody who knew the kind of life it was meant to be surrounded by?' (ii. 331). Miriam moves through the 'strange spaces' of this world of bamboo, Utrecht velvet, and Satsuma basins, faded commodities, registering its dimensions. The room appears 'old and experienced, full like her inmost mind of the unchanging past'. Despite a sense of being 'in her place in the room', amongst its odd, impenetrable dislocations, Miriam feels it will not acknowledge her. 'Nothing in her life had any meaning for it. It waited impassively for the passing to and fro of people who would leave no impression.' Here she is 'no longer a person' (ii. 334).

Through her piano-playing, Miriam tries to make her mark, to force a recognition of her own experience. 'She imagined a sonata ringing out into it, and defiantly attacked a remembered fragment. It crashed into the silence. The uncaring room might rock and sway. Its rickety furniture shatter to bits. *Something* must happen under the outbreak of her best reality' (ii. 334). She imagines the room's response: 'This dingy woman playing with the directness and decision of a man was like some strange beast.' Miriam nevertheless succeeds in discovering herself there. The room becomes tamed, domesticated, a background: 'All around her was height and depth, a sense of vastness and grandeur beyond anything to be seen or heard, yet stretching back like a sheltering wing over the past to her earliest memories and forward ahead out of sight' (ii. 335). What is at stake in these curious encounters, in Miriam's wandering through familiar and yet 'strange spaces'? Both an attempt to understand past tradition, encased and present in the opaque mystery of domestic things, and a premonition of its shattering. Miriam finds herself at home not in the secure private interior of a middle-class family, but in a room of a London boarding house, where she can enjoy 'the enviable life of a stranger' (iii. 88). Thrust out into society, she can no longer return to the parental home of the Victorian world. The question, caught up in the bee-memory of the Babington garden – where did I come from? – is also that of her modern age: 'it was a flight down strange vistas, a superfluity of wild strangeness, with a clue in one's hand, the door of retreat always open' (ii. 316).

3

A London Life

'Aren't you glad you are alive today, when all these things are happening?' (ii. 149). Miriam Henderson is referring to the new-found pleasures available to women, such as bicycle-riding. New mobilities, new freedoms. Through the eyes of its central protagonist, *Pilgrimage* explores what it meant to be a 'new woman' in the turn-of-the-century years, breaking away from familial ties, as we have seen, towards an awareness of herself as 'something new – a kind of different world'. The novel thus sketches the profile of what we might term a generational 'structure of feeling'. Miriam is located in a particular historical moment, as in some sense 'typical' of her sex and her class, living 'the ordinary average life of hundreds', in Bryher's words.[1] She exists for the reader, in a Humean sense, as a bundle of signs and impressions – inhabiting a range of references and actions strewn throughout the text which testify to its historical specificity. For the woman reader of the time, the tracing of Miriam's profile may have produced a shock of self-recognition.

Some of these clues remain easily identifiable, and are characteristic of the new-woman fiction of the period. Miriam's taste for reading Ibsen and Zola immediately marks her, as does her love for smoking cigarettes in public, her thoughts on marriage, on free love, and on riding a bicycle without a corset.

Rather more difficult to retrieve without a full-blown critical archaeology of the text is her place as a new woman within the intellectual and political milieu of the day. We are often presented with half-worked encounters with ideas, fragments of quotations, isolated moments of argumentative exchange, name-dropping, and lists of texts. We range through a narrative rich in allusions to science, philosophy, art, and religion. We visit public lectures where the focus is more on the audience reaction or Miriam's daydreaming than on the subject-matter of Dante or the photographic process.

Moreover, Miriam's own self-analysis, whether concerning her identity or her political stance, is not always consistent or reliable. At times she appears to try on ideas and labels – the range of cultural signs at her disposal – as if to discover the best 'fit'. The cultural background of *Pilgrimage* (which would, of course, include not just the years in which it is set, but also those in which it is written) seems to function as the work's unconscious archive, revealed through the parapraxes of the protagonist's actions, the dreamwork of her movements, but never as a perceivable totality. The novel thus attempts to represent the way in which an individual inevitably experiences the 'now' of his or her cultural moment as partial and unrealized, and as a changing reorientation to past events and to the pressures of the future.

It is the city landscape that proves the powerful precondition for this new woman's freedom, making possible her encounter with these different kinds of knowledge, different temporalities. Miriam's move out from the suburban family home to employment and an independent life in London is a familiar topos in fiction of the period – one example being Wells's *Ann Veronica* (1909), parodied by Richardson in *Dawn's Left Hand*.[2] Such a plot movement is an index of the social transformations that were underway. Women were being offered increased opportunities in education and new forms of waged employment. Miriam herself works variously as a governess, a teacher, and a secretary in a dental practice, while her sister Eve is a governess and a florists' assistant before managing her own shop, and her sister Harriet the landlady of a boarding house.

However caught up in the emancipatory possibilities of the times – that will to a 'self-directing, self-centered life' that Thorstein Veblen saw as a blind evolutionary reversion among the 'less manageable body of modern women' of the leisure classes[3] – these modern lives are also driven by an unrelenting economic logic. As E. J. Hobsbawm has argued:

> Some degree of women's emancipation was probably *necessary* for middle-class fathers, because by no means all middle-class families, and practically no lower-middle-class families, were sufficiently well-off to keep their daughters in comfort if they did not marry and did not work either. This may explain the enthusiasm of many middle-

class men, who would not have admitted women to their clubs or professional associations, for educating their daughters to envisage a certain independence. All the same, there is no reason at all to doubt the genuine convictions of liberal fathers in these matters.[4]

Here we have a context for Miriam's relationship with her father, that intermingling of identification and betrayal. Miriam is furnished with the means of her emancipation, but thereby enters into a social dilemma. On the one hand, she is freed through education and her father's encouragement from the constraints of her mother's generation, knowing, as 'a modern girl' – in the words of the novelist Sarah Grand – 'that a woman's life is no longer considered a failure simply because she does not marry'.[5] On the other, she has to find out the meaning of that independence for herself, in the public realm so long dominated by the values and interests of men, weighed down by the dull compulsion of the need to earn to survive – a different kind of bondage.

Miriam's predicament crucially concerns the relation of her class status to her desire for autonomy. It is no accident that the most visible forms of struggle for women's rights were confined to middle-class women of independent means. Through Miriam, Richardson explores the disjunction between the prospect of emancipation and the world of work. Smoking a cigarette in male company, 'Miriam discharged a double stream of smoke violently through her nostrils – breaking out at last a public defence of the freemasonry of women. "I suppose I'm a new woman – I've said I am now anyhow," she reflected, wondering how she would reconcile the role with her work as a children's governess' (i. 436). Brought up with the expectations of the leisure class, Miriam finds that such habits die hard: 'She did not dust, she could talk and listen, in prepared places, knowing nothing of their preparations. She belonged to the leisure she had been born in, to the beauty of things' (iii. 318). It is a life she dreams about returning to. 'The joy she had found in her invisible life amongst the servants was the joy of remaining girt and ready for the flight of return, her original nature stored up and hidden behind the adopted manner of her bondage' (iii. 245).

Like children who fantasize that their parents are not really their own but rather have stolen them away from a richer, more authentic life, Miriam has a fantasy that her 'life amongst the servants' is a matter of adoption. The truth is, of course, that

41

Miriam has to realize her independence within this working world, from which the only escape would be the unsatisfactory compromise of marriage. This is the world to which her father's actions have consigned her. There is no other avenue of return. *Pilgrimage* reveals the impact of an urban working life on a woman determined to maintain her freedom, however painful and solitary. It does so in sensuous and concrete detail: her fingernails going blue with cold in her office, her longing for the release of a teabreak, her counting of the petty cash and delight in a salary, her tired evenings. We see the misted panes of the ABC café, note the sodden feet of her sister working in the florists', and feel the hole in her shoe.

This new woman, then, experiences in her own independent life the pressures and contradictions of poverty: 'Miriam sat smarting under her own brutality ... poverty is brutalizing, she reflected miserably, excusing herself. It makes you helpless and makes sick people fearful and hateful. It ought not to be like that' (ii. 264). There is an anger in *Pilgrimage*, sometimes registered as depression, elsewhere as indignation, and increasingly in the middle volumes such as *Deadlock* as a form of political consciousness. 'Strong, cruel wealth, eating up lives it did not understand,' Miriam observes of her sister's employers. 'How did Eve manage to read *Music and Morals* and Olive Schreiner here?' (ii. 241). Miriam knows that this is a society in which unemployed governesses may commit suicide for the sake of owing rent (iii. 76). As for her own workplace, the dental practice resembles a 'family' that, when tested, reveals itself to be part of the same economic 'machinery'. From initially identifying with the employers (their world, their class), she realizes almost with surprise that her status is in fact that of a vulnerable employee. Miriam gets the sack when she speaks out:

> In the train I saw the whole unfairness of the life of employees. However hard they work, their lives don't alter or get any easier. They live cheap poor lives, in anxiety, all their best years and then are expected to be grateful for a pension, and generally get no pension. I've left off living in anxiety; perhaps because I've forgotten how to have an imagination. But that is the principle, and I came to the conclusion that no employers, however generous and nice, are entitled to the slightest special consideration. And I came back and practically said so. [...] And to prove my point individually I told him of things that were unfair to me and their other employees in the practice.

The central example of unfairness that Miriam gives her employer Mr Hancock involves their different access to a world of leisure: 'They sail off to their expensive week-ends without even saying goodbye, and without even thinking we can manage to have any sort of recreation at all on our salaries' (iii. 179). It is significant that she chooses the issue of leisure as one source of grievance, an indication of the comfortable environment from which her family has 'fallen'. More importantly, it suggests a major precondition for her access to a creative life; in her regime of work she has 'forgotten how to have an imagination'.

WHY RICHARDSON IS NOT WOOLF

Virginia Woolf's famous dictum – that a woman needs £500 a year and a room of her own in order to write – is not lost on Miriam Henderson, for whom writing and self-realization will prove much the same thing. Miriam, however, knowing the value of every pound, shilling, and penny that she earns, can only manage the latter half of the equation. And what makes *Pilgrimage* so distinctive is its refusal to let go of that fact, the consequences of the world of work, even as its aesthetic experimentation seems to lead the narrative towards a modernist transcendence of the exigencies of social life, and even as Miriam seeks out the opportunity for contemplative removal. As we will see, Richardson is no less caught up in the aesthetic pleasures offered by metropolitan experience to the leisured eye – that 'unrelented beauty', as the Imagist Amy Lowell put it, by which the city 'captures the sensuous sense of seeing'.[6] Like the Woolf of 'Street Haunting', Richardson also transforms her narrative, at times, into an 'enormous eye', registering in impressionist form the light, colour, and movement of a London street.

In 'Street Haunting' Woolf's narrator gazes with a practised dilettantism at the surface – the street and all its inhabitants, aestheticized material for her vision. The images of poverty, of people with strange names and 'curious trades', present an odd panorama, distanced and somehow consoling, for, as she concludes, 'life which is so fantastic cannot be altogether tragic'. When her vision of the beautiful is sated, this spectator can turn to the grotesquerie of those who sleep on the streets to enjoy a shiver down 'the nerves of the spine'. And, while this essay is not lacking in a degree of self-irony, knowing its privilege, acknowledging the threat it feels from 'the oddities and sufferings and sordidities' of the mass, in fact it has no means of getting below that surface, however much it indulges in a fantasy about putting on 'the bodies and minds of others ... those wild beasts, our fellow men'.[7] It may be, as Rachel Bowlby has argued, more subtly, that this is in fact what 'Street Haunting' is about: the narrator is one of the 'wild beasts' herself, whose 'imaginative freedom is qualified as that of an animal in reality tied to its place, its imaginary other identifications starting from there'. My reading may in this light ignore a degree of *rapprochement* in which 'everyone is grotesque, just as all the seeming poor can turn out from one point of view to be equivalent to affluent consumers'.[8] Not from their point of view, I would suggest. There is an inner-city primitivism at work in Woolf's essay that plays with such equivalences: metropolitan experience recast as ethnographic tour.

Interestingly it is precisely a preoccupation with surface that forms Woolf's main criticism of Richardson's *The Tunnel*, where, she argues, for all the 'vivid surface' rendered acutely through Miriam's 'touch, sight and hearing':

> sensations, impressions, ideas and emotions glance off her, unrelated and unquestioned, without shedding quite as much light as we had hoped into the hidden depths. We find ourselves in the dentist's room, in the street, in the lodging-house bedroom frequently and convincingly; but never, or only for a tantalizing second, in the reality that underlies these appearances.[9]

Yet Woolf misreads the 'surface' of Richardson's narrative, lost, as she to some extent acknowledges, without a conventional means of negotiating the kind of representation of the real that *Pilgrimage* is attempting. On one level, as I have discussed in the previous chapter, it is precisely *through* the seemingly superficial and trivial realm of everyday objects – the world of 'forgotten things' – that another dimension of reality is shown to reveal itself: a personal and collective form of memory. More importantly, here, however, is the nature of the surface rendered through Miriam's senses, which Woolf reads as a failure of Richardson's design. Miriam's consciousness is itself like a surface, a defensive layer between inside and outside, which often – in Woolf's words – 'glances off' sensations and impressions, rather than revealing hidden depths of meaning. This psychic defence recalls the kind of screening-effect I discussed earlier. Here, I am arguing, it is at once registering and intercepting the impact of Miriam's working life in the city – the consequence of that loss of home: an impact experienced both as a kind of nervous shock, capable of 'brutalizing', and as a sharpening and speeding-up of 'kaleido-scopic' perception.

In this sense the experience of the metropolitan 'surface' represented in *Pilgrimage* is very different from the vision that characterizes the dallying eye/I of Woolf's 'Street Haunting'. Miriam is tied to the dentist's room, the streets, the lodging house, in material ways. However much she might desire and occasionally achieve the luxury of Woolf's leisured perception (and, in class terms, has been educated to expect it), there is always an anxiety at her own dislocation. 'The imagination is largely the child of the flesh,' Woolf writes in her 'Memories of a Working Women's Guild'. It is for this reason that she feels unable to cross the 'impassable' barrier of the class divide, to put herself in the place of working women. 'One could not be Mrs Giles of Durham because one had never stood at the wash tub; one's hands had never wrung and scrubbed and chopped up whatever the meat may be that makes a miner's supper.'[10] Woolf can be no more than a 'benevolent spectator'; an across-class politics of solidarity among women within her work appears unimaginable.

Richardson's Miriam Henderson is, by contrast, positioned among the shopgirls and shabbiness that provide Woolf with her spectacle. Miriam must seek out her freedom by other means: through the choices she makes within the 'trampling hurry' of social life (iii. 322), and centrally through 'a *plebeian* dilettantism' (ii. 245), which is something I will discuss in more detail in the next chapter – the means by which the aesthetic of *Pilgrimage* offers its own affiliation with the experience of women's working lives. Richardson's novel is powerfully about a class dilemma and all its complex knots of identification: from Miriam's snobbery and condescension to her understanding of the pressures of a working life; from her aloof Englishness and downright anti-Semitism to her consciousness of prejudice, and recognition of the new perspectives brought to her through 'foreign eyes'. This is the struggle that is etching the 'surface' of the narrative with its difficult hieroglyphics. One way of deciphering it is to examine the way Miriam moves through the city itself.

CITY SPACES

At the beginning of *Revolving Lights* Miriam attends a socialist public meeting. The socialists or Lycurgans are just one of the groups Miriam associates with in the atomized social world of London. As she moves through the hall, Miriam registers in its uniformity an architectural ignorance of 'the wonder of moving from one space to another and up and down stairs'. This wonder becomes a metaphor for a movement between social spaces, of which the 'public platform voices' seem politically unaware, but which represents Miriam's experience of urban social life:

> Away behind, in the flatly echoing hall, was the busy planning world of socialism, intent on the poor. Far away in tomorrow, stood the established, unchanging world of Wimpole Street, linked helpfully to the lives of the prosperous classes. Just ahead, at the end of the walk home, the small isolated Tansley Street world, full of secretive people drifting about on the edge of catastrophe, that would leave, when it engulfed them, no ripple on the surface of the tide of London life. In the space between these surrounding worlds was the everlasting solitude; ringing as she moved to cross the landing, with voices demanding an explanation of her presence in any one of them. (iii. 233)

The city in *Pilgrimage* is the location of a number of discrete and clubbish social circles and groupings, each 'a single world' with its own exclusive truth. Not communities but collectivities, they are united either by a cloned 'singleness of nature' (the clannishness of aristocratic English life in Wimpole Street) or by their very transience and diversity (the Tansley Street boarding house, the numerous cafés). Moving through them, Miriam can never wholly belong. At times she experiences her mobility as a freedom, her dislocation as a vantage-point. Elsewhere it is a kind of suffering – Lukács's 'transcendental homelessness'[11] – 'was there any one, anywhere, who suffered quite in this way, felt always and everywhere so utterly different?' (iii. 315).

Miriam's experience of the city, and the contradictory affiliations it demands of her, provide a complex context for her socialist and anarchist sympathies. The task she sets herself involves at some level a utopian politics, a search for 'a vision of the future'. This she has in part learnt from her friend Hypo Wilson, 'only too glad of the opportunity of any sort of share, even as an onlooker, in the making of a new world' (iii. 252). 'A revolutionary is a man who throws himself into space,' Miriam observes, thinking of Russia. But 'in Russia there is nowhere else to throw himself?' (iii. 239). The spaces of English life appear rather more cluttered than Russia's expanses, and seem to her, moreover, 'irreconcilable'. Their interconnections are a mystery. She has to find a path for herself through them.

Urban spaces in *Pilgrimage* – streets, squares, façades, interiors – provide us with a map of a class-based social architecture through which Miriam moves, replete with all her prejudices, fears, and aspirations. More than that, they almost resemble ontological categories – an indication of different modes of being. The North London suburbia of *Backwater*, with its 'little sapling-planted, asphalt-pavemented roadways' and houses 'whose unbroken frontage was so near and so bare as to forbid scrutiny', holds a kind of terror for Miriam in its uniformity. The rooms of those whom Kracauer termed 'the sunken middle class'[12] are, in Miriam's eyes, crowded and dark, like prisons. 'To enter one of the little houses and speak there to its inmates would be to be finally claimed and infected by the life these people lived, the thing that made them what they were' (i. 289). What she fears here is a loss of a sense of the future, and a merging, undifferentiation, in the suburban mass.

In comparison, the spaciousness of 'grey, wide Bloomsbury' is an affirmation of the comfortable privilege of her childhood (iii. 244), and, as in the opening pages of *The Tunnel*, an arena for her growing autonomy. It is as open as suburbia is constricted. 'London could come freely in day and night through the unscreened happy little panes; light and darkness and darkness and light' (ii. 16). It also assures Miriam of her individuation, offering her access to 'a pathway spread throughout the world' (iii. 130). The Euston Road, which divides Bloomsbury from her northern life, is experienced as a kind of territorial boundary: 'her unsleeping guardian, the rim of the world beyond which lay the northern suburbs, banished' (ii. 15).

Of particular significance in *Pilgrimage* are those places in the city which are at once public and private: the domestic interior of the dental practice that is also a place of work; the lodging house, both home and thoroughfare; the cafés, havens of rest and places of public discussion, the retreats of working men. Places of interconnection. These spaces are central to the narrative because they present in condensed form, like the stages of small agonistic dramas, what it means in social terms for Miriam to make her journey – the passage of a woman from the domestic private interior, so long held to be the limit of her existence, into the male arena of public life. An explanation for Miriam's presence on these stages is demanded in different and often contradictory ways. Some confirm her in an already established role, according to accepted convention or tradition. This she can assume like comfortable clothing, and, in doing so, register it, perhaps for the first time, as a form of subjection. Her experience of work in Wimpole Street is one example of this. Other spaces challenge her even more fundamentally, forcing a transformation in her identity or in her perception of those around her – a metamorphosis that is either an index of her alienation, or a means by which she is freed to make the space her own. After examining the way Miriam is caught up into the spaces of her workplace, I will explore her reaction to café life as an example of this more fundamental challenging.

GOOD HOUSEKEEPING

In *The Tunnel* Richardson takes Miriam through a working day in the Wimpole Street building. Its layout suggests that of a spacious family house, even as it is a busily functioning environment, its rooms connected efficiently by a 'speaking tube'. The building's double character – both home and yet business – indicates the kind of enterprise that inhabits it. On the surface the dental practice appears an old-style concern, familial and unbusinesslike in its intimacy, where Miriam is welcome to have lunch and tea with her employers, and everyone is somehow equally in service to their aristocratic clients. Underneath, however, it is a business run on paternalistic lines, where cheerfulness is deemed part of Miriam's secretarial duty, and which is quick to remind her of her lowly status when put to the test.

During her working hours Miriam moves constantly throughout the house as if oiling the machinery of business. The movement upstairs and downstairs – which she associated in the socialist public meeting with a kind of 'wonder' – is here revealing of both the household hierarchy and the spatial network of connections that comprises her labour. In the basement is the workshop and its furnace, the lunch-room, where a woman is glimpsed scrubbing the floor, and the distant voices of servants in the 'unknown background' of the kitchens. On the other floors are the surgeries, with their rich Turkey carpets and heavy furniture, the family 'den', and Miriam's cold office. At the beck and call of every demand from the speaking tube, the relayer of messages and preparer of instruments, Miriam is the central connection of Wimpole Street life.

However, what is interesting about Miriam's position is a certain ambiguity in her status. Born into the world of her employers, she slips into their company without effort. She accompanies Mr Hancock to a Royal Institution lecture, the place her father had often visited, part of his dream of a leisured intellectual life. She accompanies Mr Orly at the piano, and helps his wife select books to read. She arranges flowers. She is consulted by Mr Hancock about the décor in his room, discussing Japanese art and its place in 'English household decoration', advice normally reserved for a female relative. Miriam is thus caught up in the domestic duties usually reserved for women in family life, playing out a role of enormous resonance in Victorian society – the housekeeper. It is a role assumed almost unconsciously:

> When she reached the hall Mr Orly's door was standing wide. Going into the surgery she found the head parlourmaid rapidly wiping instruments with a soiled serviette. 'Is it all right, James?' she said vaguely, glancing round the room.
> 'Yes, miss.' answered James [...] (ii. 43)

Yet Miriam also recognizes the exploitative seduction of such a role, for it masks, and thereby secures an altruistic dedication to, tasks which are represented as a form of domestic labour. Cleaning the dental instruments with chemical solution, Miriam reflects on the mechanical repetition of her work. 'The tedium of the long series of small, precise, attention-demanding movements was aggravated by the prospect of a fresh set of implements already qualifying for another cleansing; the endless series to last as long as she stayed at Wimpole Street.' She begins to question how people, particularly women, are brought to invest in their labour:

> Were there any sort of people who could do this kind of thing
> patiently, without minding?...the evolution of dentistry was
> wonderful, but the more perfect it became the more and more of
> this sort of thing there would be...the more drudgery workers, at
> fixed salaries...it was only possible for people who were fine and
> nice...there must be, everywhere, women doing this for people who
> were not nice. They *could* not do it for the work's sake. Did some of
> them do it cheerfully, as unto God? It was wrong to work unto man.
> But could God approve of this kind of thing?...was it right to spend
> life cleaning instruments?...the blank moment again, of gazing about
> in vain for an alternative...all work has drudgery. That is not the
> answer...Blessed be Drudgery, but that was housekeeping, not
> someone else's drudgery...(ii. 40)

Although Miriam is unable to answer the question she has
posed, the fragments of thought here circulate around the
perceived quasi-religious dedication of women's work – more
specifically, the way in which certain ideologies of femininity and
the domestic underwrite the work ethic. Miriam holds on to a
distinction between the private drudgery of housekeeping and
that of waged labour – when she later decides to make her
employers aware of their conflation of the two in their treatment
of her, she gets the sack. Yet her confusion here is partly because
she is trying to think through certain contradictions, which centre,
on the one hand, on women's work, and, on the other, on the
distinction between public and private. The problem is not only
that a discourse of women's managing of the private sphere – here
that of housekeeping – functions to insert a woman very
specifically in the wider public world of work. It is also that the
public–private distinction is breaking down before her eyes. At
the heart of the middle-class home *is* 'someone else's drudgery',
whether that dealt with by parlourmaids or cooks, or by the
women of the family themselves.

Plunged into the world of work, then, Miriam becomes
sensitized to its ramifications in women's lives. On one level the
jobs that are available to her – teacher, governess, secretary – are
all legitimated by certain naturalizing ideologies of femininity,
from those of caring and mothering to those of housekeeping. The
irony here is that the supposedly 'natural' feminine characteristics
associated with the domestic sphere are in fact exhibited by

women who are paid to do so – women, as Miriam tests out, who might choose to stop. On another, the private sphere is revealed, for some, as a workplace; for others, such as Miriam's mother, a place of waste, of 'useless' lives (i. 472). In the Wimpole Street building the contradictions of women's social status are physically brought 'home' to Miriam, and domesticity exposed as a form of ideological seduction. By assuming the role that the household makes available to her and yet maintaining a critical distance from it, she is able to question its claim, 'to avoid being shaped and branded' (iii. 245) in its image.

THE CAFÉ COSMOPOLIS

> She could understand a life that spent all its leisure in a café; every day ending in warm brilliance, forgetfulness amongst strangers near and intimate, sharing the freedom and forgetfulness of the everlasting unchanging café, all together in a common life. (ii. 394)

Café life in *Pilgrimage* holds a particular attraction for Miriam Henderson. Unlike the hierarchical arrangement of Wimpole Street, which positions Miriam very specifically in a conventional role that she must struggle against, the spaces of London cafés are levelled out – intimate thoroughfares, in which she is free to remake herself as one of a community of strangers. In the café her sense of autonomy and freedom is reinforced, only to be challenged in a more fundamental sense.

The physical boundaries of these spaces – half-retreat, half-rendezvous – seem open to metamorphosis, pervaded by mystery. In the bohemian Ruscino's 'the confines of the room were invisible', 'a vast open space of light', where, almost cinematically, 'innumerable little tables held groups of people wreathed in a brilliancy of screened light, veiled in mist, clear in sharp spaces of light, clouded by drifting spirals of smoke' (ii. 394). By contrast, in Miriam's familiar ABCs, staple eating places of her working life, the rooms suggest a solid domestic security, offering access to a warm hearth, 'a bit of her own London home', which she is always seeking out (ii. 360). Yet even the ABC is a place of secrets, a space won from the 'dark lit wilderness' of the city (ii. 76). Moreover, its walls give way osmotically to the imagination. Reading Ibsen's *Brand* in the moments of intense privacy that the public space of café life allows, Miriam is transported 'into Norway in an ABC' (ii. 384).

These places are characterized for Miriam by a shared 'secret of London', a form of freedom experienced only by those initiates who have been alone in the city. Like the boarding house, cafés confirm Miriam in her identity as a Londoner, with its curious confidence of moving at the centre of existence: 'secure from all the world that was not London, flying through space, swinging along on a planet spread with continents – Londoners' (ii. 77). For all her sense of community with these 'strong, free and untouched people', Miriam is nevertheless an outsider in the realm of the café, which emphatically belongs to men. In the ABC on the Strand she 'felt as if she were a guest of the City men' (ii. 76). And in the exotic spaces of Ruscino's she is quite transformed:

> It was a heaven, a man's heaven, most of the women were there with men, somehow watchful and dependent, but even they were forced to be free from troublings and fussings whilst they were there...the wicked cease from troubling and the weary are at rest ... She was there as a man, a free man of the world, a continental, a cosmopolitan, a connoisseur of women. (ii. 394)

To be autonomous is to become a man: café life offers Miriam the opportunity to play with such identifications, in which women might become publicly acknowledged objects of her desire.

Yet if living 'the enviable life of a stranger' here gives Miriam a certain mobility of identity, opening up a fantasy of difference and transformation, there are lines beyond which she is unable, and unwilling, to tread. These invariably involve boundaries drawn along racial lines. At times Miriam is so fundamentally challenged by the kinds of otherness she encounters in the public spaces of London that she takes obstinate and prejudiced refuge in an imperializing and xenophobic Englishness. Accompanying her Russian Jewish lover to a Docklands café, she sees a black docker eating at another table. Her response is violent in its racial and class disgust:

> Miriam sat frozen, appalled by the presence of a negro. He sat near by, huge, bent, snorting and devouring, with a huge black bottle at his side. Mr Shatov's presence was shorn of its alien quality. He was an Englishman in the fact that he and she could *not* sit eating in the neighbourhood of this marshy jungle. But they were, they had. They

would have. Once away from this awful place she would never think of it again. Yet the man had hands and needs and feelings. Perhaps he could sing. He was at a disadvantage, an outcast. There was something that ought to be said to him. She could not think what it was. (iii. 217)

Miriam's consciousness consolidates a sense of self-identity through displacement, in which a form of absolute otherness is here counterposed to what is to her a more recognizable – and hence malleable – 'alien' terrain: that of Jewishness. Michael Shatov can become 'an Englishman' by virtue of his European cosmopolitanism – 'his clear, swiftly manœuvring encyclopaedic Jewish mind' (iii. 294) – which Miriam can identify with. He is also white. Elsewhere, however, his Jewishness is an 'unmanageable burden' to her (iii. 305), and serves to underline her own English sense of self in absolute terms. His identity is at these moments to be denied.

> Looking at him with the eyes of her friends Miriam saw the Russian, standing free, beyond Europe, from the stigma of 'foreigner'. Many people would think as she had in the beginning, that he was an intellectual Frenchman, different from the usual 'Frenchman'; a big-minded cosmopolitan at any rate; a proud possession. The mysterious fact of Jewishness could remain in the background ... the hidden flaw ... as there was always a hidden flaw in all her possessions. (iii. 193)

COSMOPOLITAN LIMITS

The mapping of the metropolitan city in *Pilgrimage* thus also involves a registering of the contradictions and prejudices at the heart of the imperial nation-state which shape the desires and identifications of its subject, Miriam Henderson. It is her encounter with Jewishness which in many ways defines such a topography: it is a measure simultaneously of the idealism of Miriam's modernity and its at times blind nationalist – and xenophobic – limits. The cosmopolitanism that Jewishness represents, a form of international culture beyond national boundaries, is clearly a condition she desires. Yet she cannot imagine such a culture outside the terms of imperialism itself:

> It was an awful thought that the world might gradually become all one piece; perhaps with one language; perhaps English if those people were right who talked about Anglo-Saxon supremacy. 'England and

America together could rule the world.' It sounded secure and comforting, like a police station; it would be wonderful to belong to the race whose language was spoken all over the world. All the foreigners would simply have to become English. But that brought a dreadful sense of loss. (ii. 343)

Mr Mendizabal, who accompanies her to the café Ruscino, 'was a cosmopolitan, and he denied that there was any cosmopolis, and sympathy between races' (ii. 344). Miriam's relationship with her Jewish friends, and their 'strange knowledge', opens her eyes to her own cultural positioning, about which she feels an extreme ambivalence. Her prejudices, 'so far in you unconscious', as Michael Shatov explains, are brought unremittingly to the surface in *Pilgrimage*, there for the reader, and for Miriam herself, to confront. But, in a clearly problematic way, not to transcend or rationalize away. Miriam's coming-to-consciousness appears as a form of personal progress:

> English prejudices. He saw them as clearly as he saw that she was not beautiful. And gently, as if they were charming as well as funny to him. Their removal would come; through a painless association. For a while she would remain as she was. But even seeing England from his view, was changed; a little. The past, up to the last few moments, was a life she had lived without knowing that it was a life lived in special circumstances and from certain points of view. Now, perhaps moving away from it, these circumstances and points of view suddenly became a possession, full of fascinating interest. But she had lived blissfully. Something here and there in his talk threatened happiness. (iii. 151)

Yet, as the last lines here suggest, this is not a process that Miriam can live painlessly, without giving up the imperial 'bliss' of Englishness. While Jewishness connotes cosmopolitanism, and, indeed, a stereotypical state of homelessness (one which, for Joyce in the figure of Leopold Bloom, becomes the archetypal figure of modernist exile) which answers, in Miriam's eyes, her own deracination, it is ultimately unknowable, a threat. In a Jewish East End café, 'there were no hooked noses; no one in the least like Shylock. What were Jews? How did he know the room was full of them?' (iii. 127). Michael Shatov's anti-assimilationist Zionism, informed by the thought of Theodor Herzl,[13] is put into dialogue with Miriam's liberal-conservative defence of England's assimilationist power as Empire, of England as a 'home' for Jews: the result is the *Deadlock* of the city volume. Moreover, Michael will not rest with the cosmopolitanism she delights in:

> Frenchman, Russian, philosophical German-brained, he sat there white-faced, an old old Jew, immeasurably old, cut off, alone with his conviction, facing the blank spaces of the future. Why could he not be content to be a European? She swayed, dragging at the knot. In his deeply saturated intelligence there was still a balance on the side from which he had declared to his father, that he was first a man; then a Jew. By the accidents of living, this might be cherished. She glanced remorsefully across at him and recognized with a sharp pang of pity, in his own eyes, the well-known eyes wide open towards the darkness where she sat invisible, the look he had described … *wehmütig*; in spite of his sheltered happy prosperous youth it was there; he *belonged* to those millions whose suffering he had revealed to her, a shadow lying for ever across the bright unseeing confidence of Europe, hopeless. (iii. 168)

Entrenched in the 'whole tremendous panorama' of her Englishness, Miriam is unable to countenance the conversation discussed in the final pages of *Deadlock* which will pave the way to their marriage: she cannot embrace Judaism. Her refusal is expressed in gendered terms: it is the life of the Jewish wife and mother, destined 'to breathe always the atmosphere of the Jewish religious and social oblivion of women', that she cannot accept (iii. 224). The narrative, it appears, confirms her in her prejudice.

That *Pilgrimage* is *about* prejudice is undeniably the case: Miriam is presented as someone whose life is 'a complex system of evasions' (iii. 387); or, as Hypo puts it, 'a mass of British prejudice and intelligent obstinacy' (iii. 253). There is a complexity of positioning here that needs carefully to be discussed, with more room than I have here. Inevitably such a discussion leads to Richardson's own politics, and, specifically, her relation to the anti-Semitism endemic at the time: there is increasing evidence that Miriam's extreme ambivalences were close to her own, and put under pressure by the rise of Fascism in Germany to which she was expressly opposed. But what does it mean to *exhibit* prejudice in this way? There is a quality of confession about the unfolding of Miriam's views, as if the narrative is attempting, by virtue of its representation of coming-to-consciousness, to achieve a state of self-disinhibition. *Pilgrimage* comes close to providing 'the structure of a reflexively buffered false consciousness' which Peter Sloterdijk sees as part of the modern condition.[14] Yet it does so without its accompanying cynicism. To understand this in historical terms might mean recovering the 'shadow' of Nietzsche in Richardson's work (iii. 482); measuring *Pilgrimage* in terms of a culture which could embrace Nietzschian scepticism alongside the Christian idealism of its imperialist project. It would also be to trace the specific manifestations of what Arno Mayer has termed the 'Judeophobia' – personal prejudice – of the time, and its articulation with institutionalized and political forms of anti-Semitism.[15]

It would also be to understand the place of women in these debates, and within the culture of imperialism determining the identity of London as a metropolitan centre. It is clear that Miriam Henderson, in her intensely individualistic search for autonomy as a new woman, is continually picking her way through the possibilities open to her – religious, philosophical, institutional, political – in order to discover a means of realizing such a search. The collectivity of women she envisages, sharing the secret of independence articulated in her bee-memory, does so 'in special circumstances, and from certain points of view' (iii. 151). 'Everything depends upon a way a thing is put, and that is a question of some particular civilization,' Miriam realizes (ii. 99). Her own new-woman discourse is, for all its ventriloquating, for all its questioning, inextricably that of the metropolitan centre:

> Englishmen; the English were 'the leading race'. 'England and American together – Anglo-Saxon peoples – could govern the destinies of the world.' *What* world?...millions and millions of child-births...colonial women would keep it all going...and if religion went on there would always be all the people who took the Bible literally...and if religion were not true, then there was only science. Either way was equally abominable...for women. (ii. 252)

If *Pilgrimage* is to be understood as a search, for both a particular quality of experience and the means to represent it, then we have thus far recovered some of the dimensions of the journey. In following the ramifications of Miriam's departure from her late-nineteenth-century home into the 'stream of life' of metropolitan London, we have also been circling around a problem which Richardson's earliest critics could not work beyond: that of the novel's lack of distance from its materials, the seeming randomness of its form. *Pilgrimage* is, as I argued earlier, about the impact of modernity upon an ordinary life, and its narrative registers the shocks and euphorias of such existence. Yet if the novel comes to

celebrate the sense of 'looking with a hundred eyes, multi-
tudinously, seeing each thing from every point at once' (iii. 324),
this prospect risks a kind of scattering, an enervated emptying-out
of meaning. From where is Miriam Henderson to speak?

As we have discovered here, from a space which is
simultaneously one of prejudice and yet self-awareness. There
is, seemingly, no critical distance to be had in Miriam's processing
of the world. 'Criticism', wrote Walter Benjamin in *One-Way
Street*, 'is a matter of correct distancing. It was at home in a world
where perspectives and prospects counted and where it was still
possible to take a standpoint. Now things press too closely on
human society. The "unclouded", "innocent" eye has become a
lie.'[16] If Richardson's novel knows this, it carries on searching for a
position of distance nevertheless, via a notion of women's
experience and, centrally, its connection with cinematic form.

4

Mirioramas:
Film and Richardson

In any film of any kind those elements which in life we see only in
fragments as we move amongst them, are seen in full in their own
moving reality of which the spectator is the motionless observing
centre. [...] In life, we contemplate a landscape from one point, or
walking through it, break it into bits. The film, by setting the landscape
in motion and keeping us still, allows it to walk through us.

(CU8 184–5)

Current existence, the ultimate astonisher.

(iv. 611)

'The real English film for which so many are waiting': so Bryher
described *Pilgrimage* in 1931.[1] Films made in England at the time
were often cinematic translations of literary texts. *Pilgrimage*,
however, was never to make it on to celluloid. Instead, the novel
was imprinted by this newer medium.

In the pages of *Close Up*, an avant-garde journal on 'Film as an
Art' which charted the sudden decline of silent film and the advent
of the 'talkies' between 1927 and 1933, Richardson wrote alongside
Bryher, H.D., and the film-makers Kenneth Macpherson and the
path-breaking Sergei Eisenstein among others – about the
experience of going to the movies. Her tastes were broad – from
Westerns and melodramas to the German expressionist films of a
decade before, still showing in repertory film theatres like the
Avenue Pavilion on London's Shaftesbury Avenue. Here in film she
argued, was to be found that sense of distance so lacking in a
modern environment which 'pressed so close', in Benjamin's
words. 'In this single, simple factor rests the whole power of the
film: the reduction, or elevation of the observer to the condition that
is essential to perfect contemplation' (CU8 185).

In her columns, running under the title 'Continuous Performance' (a reference to the back-to-back screening of films which
the viewer could enter and leave at will, much as the reader of
Pilgrimage was encouraged to begin at any point), Richardson
rarely mentions specific films. Her articles are oddly abstracted
meditations, almost parables, on the potentialities opened up by
the new medium: its effects on literature, on a wider culture, and
on the existential experience available to generations who could
now never know a world without pictures. Their central concern is
spectatorship, and the form of 'contemplation' she understood
film to offer. Reading *Pilgrimage* in the light of these articles,
particularly the volumes from the 1920s onwards (the period of
her avid film-going), it is evident how often the phrases
discovered in her columns surface in her narrative and vice
versa: 'Distance *is* enchantment. It is a perpetual focus,' she writes
in a *Close Up* column in 1931 (*CU8* 183). 'Distance does not *lend*
enchantment. It shows where it is. In the thing seen, as well as in
the beholder,' Miriam muses in *Dimple Hill* (iv. 491). And again in
March Moonlight: 'Why do they say distance *lends* enchantment?
Distance in time or space does not *lend*. It reveals' (iv. 607).

What was the revelation offered by the 'perpetual focus' of film,
which she sought out in the aesthetic form of her novel? To
Richardson film was a public medium that could recover the
astonishment contained in the everyday through its 'power of
focussing the habitual'. Women, too, shared such a facility: the
ability to recognize 'the utter astonishment of life', to witness the
moment, 'before speech, when everything becomes new' (iii. 280).
Film – silent film – was thus, she argued in *Close Up*, 'essentially
feminine' (*CU10* 38). It is this parallel – between a particular
formulation of spectatorship and Richardson's representation of
women's experience – that I will now trace in *Pilgrimage*: first, in
terms of the consciousness of Miriam Henderson: and, secondly,
as a measure of the aesthetics of the novel itself.

GOING TO THE PICTURES

Miriam Henderson never visits a picture palace in *Pilgrimage*. In
her late-nineteenth-century, turn-of-the-century world, this is an
experience yet to impinge upon her. It is remarkable enough for

59

Miriam to read men's newspapers; newsreels are a distant prospect in the culture at large. Even within the streets of London such an experience for a young middle-class woman, consigned to the dark among strangers, would have at this time been unthinkable. Yet, if Miriam never goes to the pictures, the narrative itself does.

The folded narrative of the novel, both in the turn-of-the-century world and at the moment of its writing, inscribes Miriam's visual field into its own more complex one. Miriam's perspective is shaped by the visual technologies of her moment: the lantern slide and almost eponymous Mirioramas of *Honeycomb*; the photographic method of Daguerre in *The Tunnel*; the kaleidoscope and stereoscopes of her childhood remembered in *Interim* (1919). Yet the mobile impressionism of her consciousness seeks out a form adequate to its 'flight down strange vistas' (ii. 316), and in so doing anticipates the technology of the moving image that will inform this 'new mentality'. 'The logical end of impressionist art is the cinematograph,' Ezra Pound suggested.[2] Through the curious temporal telescoping of the narrative, *Pilgrimage* brings the future – the 'logical end' – to bear on Miriam's present. It becomes difficult to think of the theatre of Miriam's consciousness outside the dimensions of cinematic space:

> She was in a theatre, without walls, her known world and all her memories spread, fanwise about her, all intent on what she saw, changing, retreating to their original form, coming forward, changing again, obliterated, and in some deep difficult way challenged to renewal. The scenes she watched opened out one behind the other in clear perspective, the earlier ones remaining visible, drawn aside into a bright light as further backgrounds opened. (iii. 78)

Such an experience is, moreover, a 'common possession of all who would be still'. As she travels on a London bus, among others similarly 'alive and aware', Miriam's consciousness bears the narrative imprint of the experience of the picture palace:

> In the dimly lit little interior, moving along through the backward flowing mist-screened street lights, she dropped away from the circling worlds of sound, and sat thoughtless, gazing inward along the bright kaleidoscopic vistas that came unfailing and unchanged whenever she was moving, alone and still against the moving tide of London. (iii. 114)

Moving, and yet still: in an analogous way, for Richardson in *Close*

Up, film allowed the moving landscape to 'walk through' the motionless spectator. This narrative translation of film defines Miriam Henderson's experience as a *flâneuse*, mediating her leisurely perception of the metropolitan landscape in ways we will discover in a moment. Yet it also offers us access to a different world as I argued earlier, 'a space unconsciously interwoven', as Walter Benjamin described: the field of the optical unconscious, in which Miriam's perceptions carry inscribed within them the lineaments of deeper desires and repressions.

DREAMS AND AWAKENINGS

In 1924, Gloria Fromm tells us, Richardson reviewed *Studies in Dreams*, by Mrs H. A. Foster. The book was about the ability to produce and control 'effective dreaming'. The reviewer was unconvinced by this 'reconstruction of the dream as a controllable faculty': in any case she would much have preferred 'the chance of profound unconsciousness' to dreaming. The only time she had ever experienced such an unconsciousness was at a moment of awakening, when she had discovered herself both 'busily alive in the past, and at the same moment onlooker at [her]self living'. Her 'known self' was an 'actor' living through 'whole strands of life' simultaneously; while as spectator she could also look backwards into the past and towards the future. This, Richardson suggested, was her aim: to be in 'current possession, from a single point of consciousness, of [her] whole experience intact', and from there to be able to arrange 'the immediate future'.[3]

Miriam Henderson would seem to share this aim. Experiencing London at times as a gentle phantasmagoria of moving shapes and colours, through a 'dream-like wonder' (iii. 196), she is simultaneously inside and outside the scene, absorbed and yet aware. 'Intact', to use Richardson's word, in perhaps its unconscious sense: untouched, inviolate. But the dream landscape of London holds its horrors as well as its pleasures. On the one hand, it is a 'mighty lover, always receiving her back without words, engulfing and leaving her untouched, liberated and expanding to the whole range of her being' (iii. 272). On the other, the streets contain 'strange unconsciously noticed things' (iii. 133) which invasively threaten her well-being. Her strolling is obstructed by 'figures of men, dark,

in dark clothes, presenting themselves [...] mean and suggestive'
(ii. 96). Or by associations, such as the memory of her mother,
triggered inexplicably by an advertising sign:

> WHY must I think of her in this place?... It is always worse just along
> here... Why do I always forget there's this place... always be hurrying
> along seeing nothing and then, suddenly, Teetgen's Teas and this row
> of shops? I can't bear it. I don't know what it is. It's always the same. I
> always feel the same. It is sending me mad. One day it will be worse. If
> it gets any worse I shall be mad. Just here. Certainly. Something is
> wearing out of me. I am meant to go mad. If not, I should not always
> be coming along this piece without knowing it, whichever street I take.
> Other people would know the streets apart. I don't know where this
> bit is or how I get to it. I come every day because I am meant to go
> mad here. Something that knows brings me here and is making me go
> mad because I am myself and nothing changes me. (ii. 136)

In this passage, a complete chapter from *The Tunnel*, Miriam is
engulfed by her environment as if by her unconscious, that
something 'wearing' through her defences. Caught out, experiencing a loss of control, in the rush of street life. Underneath the
surface of people's minds, she intuits in *Interim*, 'were
...amoebae, awful determined unconscious ...octopuses
...frightful things with one eye, tentacles, poison-sacs' (ii. 317).
The danger of *Pilgrimage*, it would appear, of letting the stream of
moving shapes and mnemic images flow, involves the fear of
what lies beneath. The metaphor of the screen punctuates the
narrative with a patterning of repression and projection. Even in
the final volume, *March Moonlight*, Miriam has yet to come to
terms with the repressed store of memory: 'If one could fully
forgive oneself, the energy it takes to screen off the memory of the
past would be set free' (iv. 607). Richardson's own fascination
with, and yet refusal of, psychoanalysis is thus paralleled in the
aesthetics of her narrative. The novel privileges those moments of
awakening out of a 'profound unconsciousness', rather than the
attractions of the dream landscape, moments which suggest a
level of subjective 'screening' and thus a degree of control:

> When I open my eyes there is a certain amount of light – much less
> than I felt before I opened them – and things that make, before I see
> them clearly, an interesting pattern of dark shapes; holding worlds
> and worlds, all the many lives ahead. And I lie wandering within
> them, a different person every moment. (iii. 478)

The answer for Miriam in the troubled early volumes appears to be forgetfulness; and also to find the appropriate distance from – or proximity to – the world 'pressed so close'. The term she uses in *Revolving Lights* to describe such a stance is 'plebeian dilettantism' (iii. 245).

'PLEBEIAN' SPECTATORSHIP

'Contemplation is freedom,' Miriam muses (iii. 282). Her need for a position that will allow her to enjoy 'the marvellous quiet sense of life at first hand' (iii. 368) intensifies throughout the pages of *Pilgrimage*. It is a state she associates with solitude, silence, and a seizing of the present moment. Hers, she considers, is a 'plebeian dilettantism', one that rejects the leisured and privileged view-point of the class to which her father had aspired, in favour of a 'lively consciousness of other ways of living' (iii. 244). Miriam, as a working woman, has a more 'catholic' outlook, freeing herself for 'a wider contemplation than he would have approved' (iii. 245); one in which she is 'more and more consciously ranged on all sides simultaneously' (iii. 246).

In her strolling Miriam thus modifies the *flânerie* which in Baudelaire is the characteristic mode of aesthetic pleasure in the city – the purview of the genteel man of leisure. In *Pilgrimage* it passes through a form of nineteenth-century transcendentalism – a Whitmanesque 'loafing'[4] – which democratizes such a stance as 'the common possession of all who would be still' (iii. 114). This will connect with Richardson's discussion of the mass audience of popular film in interesting if problematic ways. As a woman, however, Miriam finds the freedom of such an attentiveness involves a certain struggle. On the one hand, it opens up, in an 'epical' form, the prospect of women's public equality. Walking through the West End, an experience denied to respectable women in the late nineteenth century, Miriam encounters an old friend: Tommy Babington. Will he acknowledge her, equal at last?

> Silent acceptance had been forced upon him by a woman of his own class. She almost danced to the opposite pavement in this keenest, witnessed moment of her years-long revel of escape. He would presently be returning to that other enclosed life to which, being a man, and dependent on comforts, he was fettered. Already in his

63

mind was one of those formulas that echoed about in the enclosed life.... 'Oui, ma chère, little Mirry *Henderson*, strolling, at midnight, across Piccadilly Circus.' (iii. 278)

On the other hand, this world of exchanged glances elsewhere positions Miriam in a more commodified economy of the streets – the object of the male gaze. It is the prostitute who becomes the female figure of independent modernity:

> One image; perceived only with the body, separated and apart from everything else. Men were mind and body, separated *mind* and *body*, looking out at women, below their unconscious men's brows, variously moulded and sanctified by thought, with one invarying eye. There was no escape from its horrible blindness, no other life in the world to live.... The leer of a prostitute was ... reserved ... beautiful, suggesting a daily life lived independently amongst the impersonal marvels of existence, compared with the headlong desirous look of a man. (iii. 208)

If 'plebeian dilettantism' notionally holds out the prospect of a form of strolling contemplation that all might enjoy in the city streets, it remains an ambivalent experience for women. And one individually realized: the public space is not their own. 'Something between a man and a woman, looking both ways' (ii. 187), Miriam's wanderings through this realm of glances are in part to find her 'secret' confirmed and shared in the recognition of others. Keeping her 'untouched strength free' (iii. 245) for such attentiveness, Miriam will succumb, at the end of *The Trap*, to exhaustion; at the end of *Clear Horizon*, to a nervous breakdown: 'Ten years. One long moment of attention, more or less strained, day and night, since the day she sat, dressed in mourning, reluctantly and distastefully considering the proffered employment' (iv. 386). The only answer is to escape from the city. A voyage out: first to the Swiss mountains of *Oberland*, and, on return, the Quaker retreat of *Dimple Hill*.

TRANSPARENCIES

> A person who, after a year in the city, spends a few weeks in the mountains abstaining from all work, may unexpectedly experience colourful images of landscape coming over or through him in dreams or daydreams.[5]

The volumes from *Oberland* on suggest a different phase of movement in the narrative of *Pilgrimage*. In terms of technique, they are cinematic in a way that contrasts with the often kaleidoscopic impressionism of the earlier volumes. *Oberland* operates in part as a nostalgic return to the epiphanic landscape of *Pointed Roofs*: though with a difference. There the 17-year-old Miriam Henderson had, from the removal of Germany, begun to exhibit and partially register the desires and identifications which shape her later life – her ambivalences and yet pleasure in the company of women, the possibilities and yet rejection of marriage. In the mountain 'dream city' of *Oberland* more than ten years later Miriam consciously makes out the shape of her desires which she will carry with her, more realized, into the 'immediate future' of her London life. The image of *Oberland* becomes a 'transparent film' over Miriam's experience in subsequent volumes, an 'Oberland life' which in its super-imposition breaks through her urban existence to allow her to read it anew.

Where film thus far has provided a language for the theatre of Miriam's consciousness and a means of articulating her percep-tions, it seems to become a more impersonal condition which the diegesis of the narrative itself aspires to in these volumes: an ordering of images in time that approaches a form of montage. Take, for example, the following passage from *Dawn's Left Hand*:

> The coming end of today's morning tapped stealthily on her mind and began to spread its influence. Just enough time for all that remained to be done. With a deep sigh that brought to her eyes a smile of salutation, she sat down at her table and gathered together the scattered letters and cheques and felt time at once resume its deep, morning quality, and turned to greet Hawkins come quietly in from the basement workshop for the mechanics' wages with the morning in his eyes. The sunlight would now be striking in through the barred basement skylight. Above the horrid gold coins, they met in silent agreement and exchanged their differently worded tributes, and parted with the cunning smiles of conspirators enriching their secret by leaving it unspoken.
>
> A glance at her clock showed its hands met on noon and, propped against its side, a letter come by the mid-morning post and placed carefully there, clear of the table's litter, by Eve, addressed to herself. In a strange hand. Queer staccato pen-strokes, sloping at various angles, with disjointed curves set between: *Amabel*.

> A mass of small sheets, covered, without margins. Strange pattern
> of curves and straight strokes rapidly set down. Each separately. Gaps
> not only between each letter but also between the straight and the
> curved part of a single letter. Letters and words to be put together by
> the eye as it went along. (iv. 214)

The reader of this passage has, like Miriam, to put together the
scene 'by the eye' as it moves along. All that 'happens' here is
clear: on one late morning Miriam is fulfilling her duties by
organizing the wages; then contemplating the letter which has
arrived from the woman who has earlier declared her love for her
by writing on her mirror. Yet the scene is broken up into a series
of images which depend particularly on the visual field opened
up by the technical development of the close-up. The effect of this
sequence is to play with the sense of time. Miriam's is habitual
action, work that has to be completed by noon – the sun is moving
through its axis through the 'barred' skylight, the hands on the
clock will meet at twelve o'clock – but the exchange of glances
and, in particular, the focus on the eyes, produces a more
languorous sense of duration: it slows the experience down. A
sense of freedom is thus hollowed out from the regimented
demands of everyday chronology.

Miriam's silent communication with Hawkins is juxtaposed
with an image of 'the horrid gold coins'. This image shocks in that
it appears a base intrusion into a mutual reverie: yet it reminds us
of the economic truth of the connection between the two of them.
The well-known Kuleshov experiment in cinematic montage,
where the image of a smile changed its significance depending on
the image preceding it, is interesting in this context. Their
expressions – first the 'smile of salutation' in Miriam's eyes, and
the 'morning' in Hawkins's eyes – are coded differently following
the image of the coins: they exhibit 'the cunning smiles of
conspirators'. The effect of bringing money into the equation is
thus to hint at a kind of material embezzlement – ironically, for
the secret they are 'enriching' involves a felt independence from
the wage economy defining their exchange.

'When the film close-up strips the veil of our imperceptiveness
and insensitivity from the hidden little things and shows us the
face of objects, it still shows us man,' Béla Balázs argued. 'For
what makes objects expressive are the human expressions
projected on to them.'[6] Miriam's response to the letter from

Amabel makes this process of projection legible. The narrative works through a series of close-ups that turn Amabel's writing into sensual hieroglyphs, suddenly massive, screen-sized, unfamiliar; needing time to be deciphered. An arena for Miriam of both fascination and desire. Writing approximates film, film approximates writing: it is this connection that will prove central to our discussion of *Pilgrimage*'s aesthetic logic. But this is, for the moment, to run ahead of my argument. How are we to understand such an approximation in terms of Miriam's relation with other women? We need to return and explore the significance of her 'Oberland life' as a clue to these hieroglyphics.

Both *Oberland* and *Dawn's Left Hand* begin with train journeys – 'as perhaps films should', Bryher comments[7] – to and from the mountains. The scenery slips past – 'a picture sliding away, soundlessly', 'pictures framed and glazed' (iv. 21) – offering Miriam the stillness in a moving landscape that for Richardson was the special provenance of film. Here such a stillness is a form of temporal removal: 'In railway stations and in trains people enter perforce their own eternity' (iv. 139). And it is a quality that defines the mountain peaks of Oberland – a 'dream city' in which she is constantly brought to the state of awakening she has been seeking: 'she awoke in light that seemed for a moment to be beyond the confines of the earth. It was as if all her life she had travelled towards this radiance, and was now within it, clear of the past, at an ultimate destination' (iv. 49).

The movement up to the transcendental heights of the mountains and back to the everyday world of London recalls a familiar topos in Romantic literature – in Wordsworth's *Prelude*, for example.[8] In such a 'phenomenology of heights and depths', as Paul de Man described it, the ascent 'resembles a state of grace although it is only the manifestation of a desire'.[9] The enclosed world of the Oberlanders is a 'Lhassa' (iv. 340) – the Tibetan Forbidden City – where Miriam has access to a state of sublime contemplation. Yet the desire manifested in such a movement is, in fact, for a release from the past that has haunted her – and, as we will see, centrally involves her sense of her own sexual identity. Such a compulsive pattern of escape and return which becomes pronounced in the later volumes – Oberland–London, Dimple Hill–London, Vaud–Dimple Hill–London – is the geographical expression of what we might see in psychoanalytical terms as a 'structuring action' shaping Miriam's psychic life. She appears to be approaching, in the 'systole and diastole' of this text, a sense of destination. Yet it remains curiously unnameable.

On her return to London from the world of *Oberland* the advertising sign for 'Teetgen's Teas' that has earlier triggered such painful memories no longer has such potency. Miriam has been freed from the weight of the past. Its gilt – guilt – letters 'bring back only the memory of a darkness and horror , to which, then, something has happened, begun to happen?' (iv. 155–6). Miriam has, it appears, achieved – momentarily - that 'possession from a single point of consciousness, of [her] whole experience intact', which Richardson associated with the concept of awakening. But what does this entail?

WOMEN AND THE BEE-MEMORY

Miriam returns from *Oberland* as someone who will take a lover. Her movements in *Pilgrimage* are testimony to another narrative, marked by prohibition: the oscillations of her desires and gender identifications refracted through the text signs of the ambivalences of her own sexual identity. Miriam is 'something new...a different kind of world'; but her difficulty in naming this newness and difference has to do in part with seeing beyond the frame of the heterosexual norms defining her womanhood – 'I hate women, and they've got to know it' (i. 436) – to find a way of articulating the 'inexpressible' 'shared being' of a love between women.

The encoding of homoerotic love in *Pilgrimage* is one dimension of Richardson's work that remains to be explored. It is what turns Amabel's script into hieroglyphs, and, by extension, the novel itself. One place to begin may be the representation of the 'bee-memory': as a founding moment of subjectivity, but also as that 'secret' which Miriam wishes to share, firstly, with her mother, and then with the imagined silent community of lonely women. It is interesting that after Oberland Miriam's *rapprochement* with the memory of her mother occurs at the same time as her reconnection with the bee-memory, her sexuality now freed to express itself: 'This person, who was about to take a lover, presently, in time, at the right time, was the one who had gazed

for ever at the flower-banks, unchanged' (iv. 178). The 'lover'
referred to most immediately is Hypo Wilson (H.G. Wells):
Miriam's affair with him results in her being 'booked for
maternity' in an ironic portrayal of Wellsian free love. Yet the
real love-affair anticipated here is with Amabel – a woman who is
'a sort of continuation of Oberland' (iv. 241), and who seems to
fulfil everything that Miriam has been searching for:

> Nothing could be better. No sharing, not even the shared being of a man
> and a woman, which she sometimes envied and sometimes deplored,
> could be deeper or more wonderful than this being together, alternating
> between intense awareness of the beloved person and delight in every
> aspect, every word and movement, and a solitude distinguishable from
> the deepest, coolest, most renewing moments of lonely solitude only in
> the enhancement it reaped by being shared. (iv. 242)

It is Amabel – as later in *March Moonlight*, it will be the more
significant yet allusive figure of Jean, herself another Oberland
(iv. 573–4) – who reconnects Miriam with that feeling of
awakening. Amabel responds to Miriam's bee-memory with
'tears of joy and sympathy' (iv. 243): the secret is shared at last.
With Amabel's recognition, Miriam comes to see herself through
the eyes of another woman, as something to be worshipped.
'There ought to be homage. There was a woman, not this thinking
self who talked with men in their own language, but one whose
words could be spoken only from the heart's knowledge, waiting
to be born in her' (iv. 230). Where Hypo Wilson can see her only
as 'an object of desire', she is, she imagines, through her own and
Amabel's eyes, marked by an 'impersonal sacredness' (iv. 231), a
madonna–mother. Sex with Hypo is for her a strange out-of-body
experience, an 'unwelcome adventure' into physical clay (iv. 257):
love between women is sublimated on to another plain, a
wordless exchange at the altar of the eternal feminine.

The melancholy of *Pilgrimage* appears to be answered here in a
fantasy which echoes the plenitude and self-sufficiency of the bee-
memory. Miriam is, significantly, both the onlooker and the object
gazed upon, her body idealized and iconic, 'a Flemish Madonna',
caught within the circle of her own desire. Her lesbian desire
concerns, in part, a narcissistic fantasy of self-origination. Such
plenitude cannot last. The loss screened by the bee-memory
returns: where Amabel will sit at the feet of Miriam as mother,
she will also take her leave. In this scenario of loss, which echoes

both the independence and yet the sorrow of the bee-memory, Miriam becomes both mother and child:

> Again and again I recalled my helpless woe when Amabel first hinted her desire for fresh people, her need to pass on, opening a gulf across which I still look back. Still, I can feel the sudden hard indifference of the wall behind us as we sat side by side across my narrow bed and, still, my own surprise at the swift tears flowing, quietly, resignedly, as though for long they had been prepared without my knowledge, for this inevitable moment, and seeming, so swiftly in that instant of silent realization had I moved back into loneliness, the witnessed grief of another. And to this day I do not know whether she desired only to test her power, or whether her response to my tears, her undertaking never to leave me, was native generosity, or just a way of comforting a child. (iv. 566–7)

If the bee-memory – as a founding moment of subjectivity – and lesbian identity come together in a complex figure in the narrative, it is a figure which is both presented and yet deflected as the novel's essential truth – as the destination of the pilgrimage. Miriam's sexual identity is couched in terms of an awakening, but it is not, to use Judith Butler's phrase, 'some primary truth awaiting its moment of true and adequate historical representation'.[10] Rather, it is produced by the choices and displacements at work in the text. Miriam's endlessly productive 'difference' continually rewrites and disrupts any such identity: the moments held out as answering an epiphanic fulfilment are turned from moments of 'grace', outside time, to scenarios marked in retrospect by the contingencies of 'desire', to recall Paul de Man's words, like brief instances of the Fall. After their intense affair, Amabel will move at Miriam's design to marry the latter's former lover, Michael Shatov; and Miriam will experience a brief yet deeper bond with the mysterious Jean in the mountains, ultimate 'friendship', even as she 'walks out' with the men of *Dimple Hill*. 'I knew', Miriam explains in retrospect, 'that in one way or another all men and women are incompatible, their first eager enthusiasms comparable to those of revivalist meetings and inevitably as transient. Only in silence, in complete self-possession, possession of the inwardness of being, can lovers fully meet' (iv. 646).

What is interesting to me, here, is that the novel makes it impossible to think of Miriam's sexual 'difference' – the identifications, self-ascribed identities, attractions, and resistances which mark her search for 'complete self-possession' – outside the historically specific conditions of her time. Motherhood, homoerotic passion, feminist and socialist militancy, solitude, the attractions of men, marriage: Miriam's journey involves repeated crossings of a well-trodden terrain for women, however much it is figured as an individual seeking of transcendence. It is the prohibitions and possibilities of her contemporary world which shape her. As Eve Sedgwick has written, in an essay on Henry James – which would illuminate Richardson's own work and her interest in him – 'models for the mutual interimplication of "homosexuality" and "heterosexuality" remain fragmentary. Perhaps, for that matter, the fragmentary is their necessary or their most becoming form. They may not be fragmentary *enough*.'[11]

WRITING

> To write is to forsake life. Every time I know this, in advance. Yet whenever something comes that sets the tips of my fingers tingling to record it, I forget the price; eagerly face the strange journey down and down to the centre of being. And the scene of labour, when I am back in it, alone, has become a sacred place. (iv. 609)

Miriam's repeated withdrawal from the intimate bonds she makes with others undoubtedly has its psychoanalytic explanation, and its own logic within the formation of her sexual identity. The book, however, accounts for this movement within the structure of the *Künstlerroman*, a novel that plots the formation of an artist: here, the passage of a writer. Within such a formation, there is often a structuring thematic of exile. In *Pilgrimage* this manifests itself less through the geographical and cultural flight suggested by Joyce's *Portrait of the Artist as a Young Man*, though the kind of escape Miriam is seeking does include her geographical removal. Exile in Richardson's novel is more a condition the woman writer has to negotiate, if she is to 'realize' from the margins all that her culture leaves out. Such a stance is, of course, problematic, since, while *Pilgrimage* often seeks to locate women in essentialist terms 'outside' the masculine chatter of the dominant culture, Miriam Henderson is simultaneously positioned firmly within the

71

imperial heartland.

Estrangement from home is nevertheless where the first volume, *Pointed Roofs*, begins – it is associated with autonomy even as it inaugurates a form of mourning – but it is also seen in some sense a cognitive necessity. It marks, for example, the temporality of Richardson's notion of 'awakening': 'Busily alive in the past, and at the same moment onlooker at [her]self living.' Miriam must be both inside and outside, part of life and yet its spectator, simultaneously, in order to write.

Such a split is testimony to the dissociation of language and experience which is integral to modernity. In *Pilgrimage* this dissociation is always at the forefront of Miriam's understanding of culture, undermining her inherited beliefs: '*All* that has been said and known in the world is in *language*, in words [. . .]. Then no one *knows* anything for certain' (ii. 99). It also provides a means of theatricalizing her sense of the difference between the experience of men and women. 'Man's life was bandied to and fro ... from *word* to *word*. Hemmed in by women, fearing their silence, unable to enter its freedom – being himself made of words – cursing the torrents of careless speech with which its portals were defended' (iii. 278). Women speak a different experiential language: *Pilgrimage* in this sense sees itself as a massive work of translation. 'That is the curse of speech,' Miriam explains to Hypo, 'its inability to express several things simultaneously. All the unexpressed things come round and grin at everything that is said. One day I shall become a Trappist' (iv. 164). Silence and simultaneous expression: this is the paradoxical aim of the narrative, which seeks out alternative 'alphabets' in its attempt to represent women's experiential 'freedom'.

ALPHABETS

In her useful reading of *Pilgrimage* as a precursor of *écriture féminine*, Jean Radford suggests that, in its quest to represent female subjectivity, the narrative – and Miriam Henderson herself – seek out 'an alternative symbolic universe'. I agree, though I want to explore this question from a rather different perspective. Miriam's throwaway remark about becoming a Trappist – a religious order predicated on the vow of silence – indicates one kind of choice she repeatedly makes in the final volumes: to enter different 'closed' communities where she can establish the 'sacred space' for her writing, as if there exists a pre-given collectivity, somewhere, where the dissociations of language and experience can be overcome.

'Exile' in *Pilgrimage* thus also connotes a quasi-spiritual choice of a contemplative life rather than an active one. Yet it is not straightforwardly realized. Miriam experiences it as a 'tug-of-war' within her. In the sublime 'Lhassa' of Oberland she finds herself arguing in socialist terms about property and rent, while in London, witnessing Amabel's militancy, she moves away from activism. In the 'enclosed world' of the Quaker community of Dimple Hill, she comes close to finding what she has been searching for:

> Their alphabet, their way of handling life, I mean the business of minute to minute living in the spirit which gives them their perspective and their poise and serenity, is the best I've met. But the thought of the missing letters makes the idea of a Quakerized world intolerable. And the thought of a world without Quakers is equally intolerable. (iv. 603)

Even here there is something missing. Miriam's experience among the Roscorlas reveals that there are different languages of silence: 'silences beyond those proscribed by Quakerly technique' (iv. 611). Her interactions with the community reveal deeper, unspoken desires and allegiances as conventional in patriarchal terms as the familial world she has left behind. As a prospective sister-in-law Miriam is regarded as a man's 'property', and her staunch independence produces dislocations. Her 'profanity' makes her an outsider even as she expresses a 'blind longing' for membership. She will continue to visit Dimple Hill, however, as a place for her writing. The woman of the future, Richardson suggests in *Vanity Fair*, will become 'within the council of nations what the Quaker is within the council of religions' (WF 40).

What are the letters missing from this alphabet that is a 'way of handling life'? Like the earlier writing from Amabel, they are those which lead her to another woman, 'making her, and not the letter, the medium of expression' (iv. 215). The woman who

73

embodies such a transfiguration from letter – increasingly understood as spiritual letter, or logos – into life, is Jean, whom Miriam meets in Vaud, another Oberland. Jean is, as Miriam points out ecstatically, her 'clue to the nature of reality' (iv. 612). She 'lives in a world she sees transfigurable. Already for her, transfigured. What comes to others only at moments is with her always ...' (iv. 579). Jean's embodiment of an unconditional love, all-encompassing and yet prepared to relinquish everything – 'Hadst thou stayed, I must have fled' (iv. 575) – represents the perfect articulation of the freedom of the bee-memory and the sublimation of its loss. She can be read as a culmination of Miriam's journey understood as religious quest – placing the novel within a tradition of feminine mysticism, as both Stephen Heath and Jean Radford have argued. Yet, no less as part of that tradition, she is also a hieroglyphic within the narrative of a love which dare not speak its name:

> If I were less than I am, I should talk about her until my friends would grow to dread her name. If I were more than I am, I should follow her path, the path to freedom. But I forget. Again and again, until something pulls me out into remorse. If only I could remain always in possession of my whole self, something of Jean-in-me would operate
>
> Good that she is gone. How right are the Catholics in separating within their orders those who grow too happy in each other. To give oneself, fully, to God-in-others, one must belong to no one. Careful though she was, and in the end taught me to be, to avoid, in public, any revelation of partiality, we yet aroused jealousies. As those last weeks slid away, the glow we created in each other could not be concealed. (iv. 612)

Again, the image of a religious order is used to name this ideal sisterhood. Significantly, however, the language of spiritual 'revelation' is here caught up in another kind of disclosure: that of a love between women which Miriam is 'taught' to conceal, the name that others may 'dread'. Jean is the enigmatic crossing point between the religious and sexual discourses of the text, a transfiguration of the eternal, word made flesh. Lesbian love, universalized as the 'shared being' of relations between women, becomes *the* vehicle of redemption, yet is glimpsed only in signs and epiphanic moments; its prohibition in religious terms, a worldly failure, a mark of the Fall. Where Jean embodies this truth, Miriam transfigures it in another way: 'Her light footsteps died away down the corridor, leaving me alone with the realization of a bond, closer than any other, between myself and what I had written' (iv. 611).

There is seemingly a paradox at work. The state that Miriam aspires to as a model of futurity – the language of a woman yet to be born in her, for which she is searching through membership of an imagined community of women – always already exists. It is a 'reality' she struggles to remember even as it is yet to be realized. A modernist crisis is thus recast in terms of women's cultural history. The forgetting she experiences suggests a wider amnesia: the difficulty, as Richardson put it, of 'think[ing] the feminine past' outside its patriarchal mediation. Yet modernity offers, through its 'revelations' in the lives of a 'new type' of woman, the opportunity of a different kind of remembering, a realignment and community with that unspoken past. The prospect of fulfilment through the 'wreckage' of tradition, now broken open. Richardson's essentialist construction of 'the feminine' is thus a complex strategy, at once an encrypting of a desire which cannot be named, utopian in its search for a women's 'Lhassa' within the everyday, and a form of cultural re-evaluation. The 'Now' time which Miriam seeks out, that moment of awakening which gathers up past, present, and future in a cessation of what she calls 'becoming', is a women's time. As Richardson herself wrote in 'Women and the Future':

> For the womanly woman lives, all her life, in the deep current of eternity, an individual, self-centred. Because she is at one with life, past, present, and future are together in her, unbroken. Because she thinks flowingly, with her feelings, she is relatively indifferent to the fashions of men. [...] Only a complete self, carrying all its goods in its own hands, can go out, perfectly, to others, move freely in any direction. Only a complete self can afford to man the amusing spectacle of the chameleon woman. (WF 40)

If *Pilgrimage* attempts to display the 'spectacle of the chameleon woman' in its endless Mirioramas, it does so within its own search for Now-time in a complex act of memory. It is the novel that aspires to the condition of the 'complete self'. Yet, just as Miriam, a new-formed writer, must discover the missing letters of her alphabet that will connect her to such experience, the narrative must also find an alternative symbolic language: one making women, 'and not the letter, the medium of expression'. The language of film.

75

FILM: *PILGRIMAGE*'S END?

> And the film, regarded as a medium of communication, in the day of
> its innocence, in its quality of being nowhere and everywhere,
> nowhere in the sense of having more intention than direction and
> more purpose than plan, everywhere by reason of its power to evoke,
> suggest, reflect, express from within its moving parts and in their
> totality of movement, something of the changeless being at the heart of
> all becoming, was essentially feminine. (*CU*10 36)

We have already begun to read the narrative of *Pilgrimage* in
cinematic terms. Film offers a visual syntax – of flashbacks, close-
ups, dissolves, montage – with which to order the flow of images
in the text, a stream 'put together by the eye'. On one level, the
subjective space occupied by the novel's presiding consciousness
is opened up as a visual field – one marked by unconscious
desires and repressions as well as a kaleidoscopic impressionism.
The realm of the optical unconscious leads us not simply into the
reaches of Miriam's identity, but also out into the history that is
shaping her, in which the psychological 'structuring action' of one
woman's leave-taking is representative of the experience of
modernity itself.

On another level, film is present in this 'folded' narrative in
almost utopian terms: as a future that the text is aspiring to even
as its possibility is mined in the present. Richardson hailed film as
'the art-form of the future' in *Close Up*, one that promised to bring
a particular form of aesthetic contemplation to a popular
audience. Its power, she argued, was in 'mirroring the customary
and restoring its essential quality': an awakening from 'the state of
deadness to the habitual' (*CU*8 183). In this sense a parallel can be
drawn between the presence of film in the narrative and Miriam
Henderson's own experience of moments of 'awakening' as
glimpses of the future state she is journeying towards. It is this
parallel I want to explore in more detail in this final section.

Writing, then, in the narrative of *Pilgrimage*, finds its
equivalence in film. Miriam writes in 'word-pictures' (iv. 611).
Imagination, she decides, involves a particular relationship to the
image: 'Imagination means holding an image in your mind. When
it comes up of itself, or is summoned by something. Then it is not
outside, but within you. And if you hold it, steadily, for long
enough, you could write about it forever' (iv. 613). Yet Miriam is

just setting out as a writer. Hers is a rather static conception, which the narrative has itself long surpassed. Film, Richardson writes, 'by setting the landscape in motion and keeping us still, allows it to walk through us' (*CU*8 185): it is the turn-of-the-century landscape that we see walking with considerable dynamism through Miriam Henderson, leaving its difficult hieroglyphics for the reader to decipher.

Writing finds its equivalence in film; yet film, in Richardson's terms, can also echo a form of modernist writing, rousing the spectator's 'collaborating creative consciousness'. In her *Close Up* columns she argued against the criticism which saw the movies as a mass cultural 'dream-world' and 'opiate' that produced in its audience a state of anaesthetized distraction. Richardson finds in films of all kinds a critical potential to the extent that they offer, to varying degrees, a form of aesthetic contemplation:

> Is there not a certain obscenity [...] in regarding pictures we despise and audiences we look down upon in their momentary relationship as we imagine it to exist in the accursed picture-house? Should we not rather set ourselves the far more difficult task of conjuring up the pre-picture outlook on the life of those who make no contact with art in any form, and then try to follow out in imagination the result of innumerable gifts of almost any kind of film, bestowed along with it, unawares, and therefore remaining with the recipient all the more potently: the gift of quiet, of attention and concentration, of perspective? The social gifts: the insensibly learned awareness of alien people and alien ways? The awakening of imaginative power, the gift of expansion, of moving, ever so little, into a new dimension of consciousness. (*CU*9 307)

Film spectatorship is here seen as a transformative experience, centred on the possibility of 'awakening'. 'Almost any kind of film' brings about this collaboration between the unconscious and conscious which she notes elsewhere is 'the condition ruling all great art' (*CU*5 55; CBP 161). Yet there are distinctions to be made between the different forms of script on offer. In 'Pictures and Films' Richardson compares the 'movies' or 'pictures' to the 'the FILM' in a way that rehearses the divide between mass cultural forms and modernist art. While 'movies' are no less 'food' for a 'discriminating' mind that the film 'art-form', they present no more than innumerable 'snap-shot records'. Refusing to label them 'infantilizing', as some critics had done, Richardson nevertheless reads in them a 'child-like trust' in the world – in a way that might recall the happiness of the bee-memory without its accompanying loss: 'the battles and the problems of those who trust life are not the same as the battles and problems of those who regard life as the raw material for great conflicts and great works of art' (*CU*5 57). Film has a critical potential, then, to the extent that it becomes art: thus the project of *Close Up* itself is revealed, setting out in 1927 as 'a monthly magazine to begin the battle for film art'.

If film can be seen as a modernist writing, marked by conflict and difficulty, it also for Richardson contains the potential for reconciliation. Film of all kinds, is a vehicle for an experience resembling the 'plebeian dilettantism' – transcendental 'loafing' – that Miriam Henderson seeks out in her pre-picture world of the 1890s in *Pilgrimage*. Richardson's columns constantly refer to a vision of potential community which breaks beyond the narcissistic confines of such an experience:

> Must we not, today, emerge from our small individual existences and from the narcissistic contemplation thereof? Learn that we are infinitesimal parts of a vast whole? Labour and collaborate to find salvation for a world now paying the price of various kinds of self-seeking?
> [...] But the everlasting WE who is to accomplish this remains amidst all change and growth a single individual. (*CU*8 183)

Such a vision suggests the optimism of a Christian socialism, which could celebrate the coming of cinema to the slums and 'every parish', as a democratizing of access to 'the living news of the changing world'. There is an almost Wellsian utopian delight in the prospect of creating 'world-citizens' – yet one that is marked, as Rebecca Egger has suggested, by an expansionist rhetoric.[12] On one level, film seemed to herald a form of internationalism – which, as we found in *Pilgrimage*, is often couched for Richardson in imperialist language – demonstrating, as H. D. wrote, that 'we are no longer nations. We are or should be a nation.'[13] On another, it is seen in elevated terms as a path to collective salvation. The film audience, in Richardson's columns, often appears as a 'congregation', the film as a eucharistic form of 'bread'; while in the picture palace 'never before was such all-embracing hospitality save in an ever-open church'. 'Let us by all means confess our faith,' she writes in 'The Thoroughly Popular

Film' in 1928. 'In this case faith in Art as an ultimate, a way of salvation opposed, though not necessarily contradictory, to other ways of salvation' (CU4 48).

In 1928 this confession of faith suggests an optimism which was soon to be shattered. *Close Up* was to run until 1933, the year that Hitler became Chancellor of Germany, when the first concentration camps were established for political prisoners. In June of that year, Bryher wrote in an article entitled 'What shall you Do in the War' of the political torture and the persecution of the Jews taking place in a Berlin which still had its unwitting tourists. To a left magazine that had always looked to the avant-garde of Germany and Russia, discussing workers' film movements and Eisenstein's dialectical materialism as well as the latest programme from the Avenue Pavilion, the situation in Germany was of immense concern. And, in cinematic terms, across the Atlantic the talkies had arrived in 1929 with a speed 'as sudden as a Mexican rebellion' in which the advent of the voice was to reinforce the sense of national cultural boundaries. The vision of internationalism was under pressure.

It may be that Dorothy Richardson's scepticism about the talkies – the 'film gone male' as she put it in 1932, now for her inevitably 'a medium of propaganda' and a battleground – was informed by this changing political context. What is clear is that the experience of silent film came closest to the state Miriam Henderson values in *Pilgrimage*, and that, even as Richardson acknowledges its passing in the *Close Up* columns with a degree of nostalgia and regret, she had incorporated its form into the aesthetics of her narrative. The importance of silent cinema lies not just in her view that 'life's "great moments" are silent' (CU7 200), but that, as in the novel, such 'intensity of being' is a mode of experience associated with a community of feeling among women. As Anne Friedberg puts it, 'for the film to have "gone male" there had to be *a film once female*'.[14]

The picture palace, as Miriam Hansen's work has shown definitively, resembled in the early decades of the century a women's public sphere – both a place of refuge from a world of domestic drudgery and a realm that confirmed women's increasing social empowerment in its acknowledgement of the female gaze as an end in itself. As Hansen explores, cinema presented a historical challenge 'to the gendered hierarchy of private and public spheres' and marked 'women's massive ascendance to a new horizon of experience' – a horizon that was to be simultaneously inscribed, by way of defensive reaction, back into a 'patriarchal choreography of vision' even as it remained potentially in excess of such a choreography.[15] If the mode of women's spectatorship – often understood in terms of its over-identification with, proximity to, the image – was increasingly aligned with a consumerist logic, it was not wholly rationalized by it. Such a gaze – one that, in Mary Ann Doane's words, 'hovers over the surface of the image, isolating details which may be entirely peripheral in relation to the narrative'[16] – may, Hansen argues, 'feed on other registers of time and experience, linked to involuntary processes in the spectator's head – the register of the "optical unconscious"'. It thus should be theorized as 'a historically significant formation of spectatorship'.[17]

Dorothy Richardson's work – and the interaction between her writings on film and the narrative of *Pilgrimage* – could usefully be read in the light of these debates. Her concept of 'plebeian dilettantism', in particular, with its seemingly populist drive towards 'a lively consciousness of other ways of living' – echoed in the 'awareness of alien people and alien ways' which Richardson felt had been opened up by film (*CU9* 307) – is itself marked by contradictory sexual and racial configurations of female spectatorship which need more careful historical analysis.

It is clear that Richardson saw the cinema as a woman's space. One Monday afternoon, as she writes in 1927, she found herself in a dilapidated picture palace on a North London street:

> It was Monday and therefore a new picture. But it was also washing day, and yet the scattered audience was composed almost entirely of mothers. Their children, apart from the infants accompanying them were at school and their husbands were at work... Tired women, their faces sheened with toil, and small children, penned in the semi-darkness and foul air on a sunny afternoon. There was almost no talk. Many of the women sat alone, figures of weariness at rest. Watching these I took comfort. At last the world of entertainment has provided, for a few pence, tea thrown in, a sanctuary for mothers, an escape from the everlasting qui vive into eternity on a Monday afternoon. (*CU1* 35–6)

'Eternity' is thus realized in a temporary escape from washing day: film offering the weary the opportunity of contemplative distance, the 'movement that is perfect rest', as Miriam describes it in *Pilgrimage* (iv. 282). Yet how are we to read this example? Is cinema valued here, as Egger argues, as 'a technology of forgetfulness'?[18] Or are we to understand this 'escape' as the registering of another horizon of experience, no less social in meaning for its distance from the everyday, 'forgetfulness' as a catachrestical naming of a certain mode of reception?

Elsewhere, women's movie-going – that 'unprecedented mobilization of the female gaze', as Hansen puts it[19] – is portrayed in more powerful and excessive terms. Richardson describes the encounter between an audience of chattering women and the image of a female star:

> It is not only upon the screen that this young woman has been released in full power. She is to be found also facing it, and by no means silent, in her tens of thousands. A human phenomenon, herself in excelsis [...] For all her bad manners that will doubtless be pruned when the film becomes high art and its temple a temple of stillness [...] she is innocently, directly, albeit unconsciously, upon the path that men have reached through long centuries of effort and thought. She does not need [...] the illusions of art to come to the assistance of her own sense of existing. Instinctively she maintains a balance, the thing perceived and herself perceiving. (*CU*3 52, 54)

Richardson is almost sardonically critical in this column, at the prospect of 'the dreadful woman asserting herself in the presence of no matter what grandeurs' (*CU*3 55). But there is also a fascination here. In this account the young woman is positioned within a narcissistic relation to the image: both 'the thing perceived and herself perceiving'. Yet she refuses to be trapped within it. The consumerist logic of this connection is broken, interestingly, for she 'does not need ... the illusions of art to come to the assistance of her own sense of existing'. Rather, 'she maintains a balance'. The woman spectator is, 'instinctively', in control. And bad mannered – 'profane', in the words of Miriam Henderson. The impression here is of a voluble female audience of 'tens of thousands' who refuse to be contained by the image of the feminine that confronts them, all embarked on a journey towards self-realization.

In these scenarios Richardson rehearses alternative views of women's experience of modernity as mediated by cinema. In the first, women 'escape' the demands of the everyday and compensate for its limitations and their own powerlessness

81

through a contemplative distancing. In the second, their experience is marked by a restless distraction and proximity to the image. Yet the perceptual possibilities of spectatorship suggested here go beyond the characteristic projections of the effect of mass culture on women at the time, to acknowledgements of women's 'full power' and alternative configurations of time.

To think of the narrative of *Pilgrimage* in terms of what I have been arguing as its literal in-corporation of film may be to reveal it as an extended wish-fulfilment: modernist écriture conjuring up an image of a mass audience as an ideal community that it can never possess. In this sense the novel as a form mourns its 'lost' wholeness even as it rehearses and celebrates its autonomy, projecting its lack on to cinema's *promesse de bonheur*. Perhaps. And, by the same token, we might want to read Richardson's valorization of this epiphanic state – silent, eternal, still, contemplative – as an act of removal from the 'trampling hurry' of social life, rather than a *rapprochement* with it (though no less social in meaning for all that). Both, I think are true; yet we might want to understand these readings in terms of Richardson's epic attempt to represent women's experience in historical terms. For me, film provides a space of imaginative negotiation in Richardson's work, whereby the private dimensions of one individual's self-realization resonate in terms of a wider public horizon of experience. The mobile impressionism of *Pilgrimage* subjects its world to a form of optical testing in a manner that does indeed suggest 'a historically significant formation of spectatorship'. In one woman's quest for a relationship to the image that articulates her sense of self – 'the thing perceived and herself perceiving' – we witness a continual refusal of the 'patriarchal choreography of vision' which attempts to define it. The notion of awakening, central to Richardson's novel and to her experience of film, is her own naming of that relation as a form of women's Now-time, a complex act of memory: in which the past of women's experience is broken open, continually, on to its future. In this sense *Pilgrimage*, as Richardson knew, could only ever be unfinished.

Notes

PROLOGUE

1. Bertolt Brecht, 'About the Way to Construct Enduring Works', *Bertolt Brecht Poems, Part II*, ed. John Willett and Ralph Mannheim (London: Eyre Methuen, 1976), 193. Brecht once proposed Richardson as a possible translator of his work.

CHAPTER 1. CONTINUOUS PERFORMANCE

1. Winifred Bryher (W.B.), '*Dawn's Left Hand*', *Close Up*, 8/4 (1931), 337.
2. John Cowper Powys, *Dorothy Richardson* (1931) (London: Village Press, 1974), 20.
3. Bryher, '*Dawn's Left Hand*', 337.
4. Ibid.
5. Lawrence Hyde, 'The Work of Dorothy Richardson', *Adelphi*, 2 (1924), 512.
6. Ibid. 515.
7. May Sinclair, 'The Novels of Dorothy Richardson' (1918), in Bonnie Kime Scott (ed.), *The Gender of Modernism* (Bloomington, Ind.: Indiana University Press, 1990), 444. Hyde's article would seem to be a response to Sinclair's assertion of 'the sheer depth of her plunge'.
8. Hyde, 'The Work of Dorothy Richardson', 516, 517.
9. Virginia Woolf, *A Writer's Diary*, ed. Leonard Woolf (London: Hogarth Press, 1959), 23.
10. Rebecca West, *The Return of the Soldier* (London: Virago, 1980), 25, 187, 188, 14.
11. Taken from Walter Benjamin's reading of Freud's *Beyond the Pleasure Principle*, in 'On Some Motifs in Baudelaire', in *Illuminations*, ed. Hannah Arendt, trans. Harry Zohn (London: Fontana/Collins, 1973), 162.
12. Those who were seen to have German sympathies were often hounded during the war, most notoriously D. H. Lawrence and his

wife, Frieda. Katherine Mansfield had refused to allow her satirical portraits of the German bourgeoisie, *In a German Pension*, to be reissued at this time; partly because of the contribution it would make to anti-German feeling. No such sentiment registers in the early reviews of Richardon's work, however, as far as I am aware.

13. Fredric Jameson, *Modernism and Imperialism* (Derry: Field Day, 1988), 10.
14. E. M. Forster, *Howards End* (Harmondsworth: Penguin Books, 1989), 74.
15. Jameson, *Modernism and Imperialism*, 12.
16. From a letter to Bryher thanking her for the gift of five volumes of Proust, quoted in Rachel Blau DuPlessis, *Writing Beyond the Ending: Narrative Strategies of Twentieth-Century Women Writers* (Bloomington, Ind.: Indiana University Press, 1985), 235 no. 21.
17. Walter Benjamin, 'The Image of Proust', in *Illuminations*, 205.
18. Walter Benjamin, 'On Some Motifs in Baudelaire', in *Illuminations*, 161.
19. Marcel Proust, *Remembrance of Things Past*, xii. *Time Regained*, trans. Stephen Hudson (London: Chatto and Windus, 1949), 238–9.
20. Gilles Deleuze and Félix Guattari, *What is Philosophy?*, trans. Graham Burchell and Hugh Tomlinson (London: Verso Books, 1994), 176. Thanks to John Kraniauskas for bringing this work to my attention.
21. Virginia Woolf, 'Dorothy Richardson', in *Women and Writing* ed. Michèle Barrett (London: Women's Press, 1979), 191.
22. Deleuze and Guattari, *What is Philosophy?*, 168.
23. John Ruskin, *The Stones of Venice*, in *Collected Works*, ed. E. T. Cook and Alexander Wedderburn (London: George Allen, 1903), ix. 403.
24. John Ruskin, 'The Lamp of Memory', repr. in Michael Wheeler and Nigel Whiteley (eds.), *The Lamp of Memory: Ruskin, Tradition and Architecture* (Manchester: Manchester University Press, 1992), 229.
25. Rosalind Krauss, ' Photography and the Simulacral', *October*, 31 (1984), 57.
26. Siegfried Kracauer, 'Photography', trans. Thomas Y. Levin, *Critical Inquiry*, 19 (1993), 432.
27. Roland Barthes, *Camera Lucida: Reflections on Photography*, trans. Richard Howard (London: Fontana, 1984), 90.
28. Hyde, 'The Work of Dorothy Richardson', 512.
29. In a letter from Roger Fry to Virginia Woolf, quoted in Rosalind Krauss, *The Optical Unconscious* (Cambridge, Mass.: MIT Press, 1993), 126.
30. Ibid. 118.
31. A point I have explored further in 'Releasing Possibility into Form: Cultural Choice and the Woman Writer', in Isobel Armstrong (ed.), *New Feminist Discourses* (London: Routledge, 1992), 83–102.
32. Cor. nent prefacing her article, 'The Role of the Background: English Visitors to the Swiss Resorts during the Winter Sports Season', *Sphere*, 99 (1924), 226.

33. Gloria Fromm, *Dorothy Richardson: A Biography* (Urbana, Ill.: University of Illinois Press, 1977), 397.
34. Kenneth Macpherson, 'As Is', *Close Up*, 2/2 (1928), 8.

CHAPTER 2. SCREEN MEMORIES

1. From Walter Benjamin, *Das Passagen-Werk*, quoted and translated by Susan Buck-Morss in her *The Dialectics of Seeing: Walter Benjamin and the Arcades Project* (Cambridge, Mass.: MIT Press, 1989), 279.
2. Virginia Woolf, *To the Lighthouse* (Oxford: World's Classics, 1992), 87.
3. May Sinclair, *A Defence of Idealism* (1917); quoted in Suzanne Raitt, *Vita and Virginia: The Work and Friendship of Vita Sackville-West and Virginia Woolf* (Oxford: Clarendon Press, 1993), 120.
4. Raitt, *Vita and Virginia*, 132. Raitt's reading of women's mysticism within a lesbian context and tradition in chapter 5 of her book is an invaluable way of beginning to think about religious consciousness in *Pilgrimage*.
5. Letter from Dorothy Richardson to Shiv K. Kumar, 10 Aug. 1952. Quoted in his 'Dorothy Richardson and the Dilemma of "Being versus Becoming"', *Modern Language Notes*, 74 (1959), 495.
6. Raitt, *Vita and Virginia*, 141.
7. Walter Benjamin, quoted in Buck-Morss, *The Dialectics of Seeing*, 265.
8. Fromm, *Dorothy Richardson*, 210. Fromm suggests that Richardson had been a keen cinema-goer from at least 1921, her writing on film beginning with the first issue of *Close Up* in 1927.
9. Walter Benjamin, 'The Work of Art in the Age of Mechanical Reproduction', in *Illuminations*, 238.
10. Ibid.; I prefer the clarity of the translation of Buck-Morss, *The Dialectics of Seeing*, 267.
11. Sigmund Freud, 'Beyond the Pleasure Principle', in *On Metapsychology* (Harmondsworth: Penguin, 1991), 285.
12. Ibid. 296.
13. Sigmund Freud, 'Childhood Memories and Screen Memories', in *The Psychopathology of Everyday Life*, standard edn., vi (London: Hogarth Press, 1960), 47–8.
14. D. H. Lawrence, 'Surgery for the Novel – or a Bomb' (1923), quoted in Stephen Heath's excellent 'Writing for Silence: Dorothy Richardson and the Novel', in Susanne Kappeler and Norman Bryson (eds.), *Teaching the Text* (London: Routledge & Kegan Paul, 1983), 126.
15. Theodor Adorno, 'Short Commentaries on Proust', in *Notes to Literature*, i., ed. Rolf Tiedemann, trans. Shierry Weber Nicholsen (New York: Columbia University Press, 1991), 174–5.

16. For a discussion of Freud's concept in relation to *Pilgrimage*, see Jean Radford, *Dorothy Richardson* (Hemel Hempstead: Harvester Wheatsheaf, 1991), 121–2.
17. Max Unold, quoted by Walter Benjamin in 'The Image of Proust', in *Illuminations*, 206.
18. Radford, *Dorothy Richardson*, 96.
19. Ibid.
20. André Green's discussion of the 'dead mother' in terms of the death of an imago in a child's mind following maternal depression is useful in this context: ' the dead mother, contrary to what one might think, is a mother who remains alive but who is, so to speak, psychically dead in the eyes of the young child in her care.' He continues: 'the consequence of the real death of the mother – especially when this is due to suicide – is extremely harmful to the child whom she leaves behind. One can immediately attach to this event the symptomatology to which it gives rise, even if the analysis reveals later that the catastrophe was only irreparable because of the mother–child relationship which existed prior to her death.' See Green's 'The Dead Mother' in his *On Private Madness* (London: Hogarth Press and Institute of Psychoanalysis, 1986), 142. Thanks to Alison Mark for bringing this work to my attention.
21. Michel Foucault, 'Of Other Spaces', *Diacritics*, 16/1 (1986), 26.
22. Virginia Woolf, 'Women and Fiction', in *Women and Writing*, 52.
23. Raymond Williams, *The English Novel from Dickens to Lawrence* (London: Chatto & Windus, 1973), 130.
24. Bryher, '*Dawn's Left Hand*', 337.

CHAPTER 3. A LONDON LIFE

1. Bryher, '*Dawn's Left Hand*', 338.
2. Richardson parallels the scenes in *Ann Veronica* where the eponymous heroine fights off the advances of Ramage, a businessman and friend of the family, in her staging of the attempted seduction of Miriam by Hypo Wilson (a fictionalized H. G. Wells). For a discussion of this scene, and Richardson's critique of the 'hideous, irritating, meaningless word *novvle*' (iv. 239) represented by Wells's fiction, see Stephen Heath, 'Writing for Silence'.
3. Thorstein Veblen, *The Theory of the Leisure Class: An Economic Study of Institutions* (London: Unwin Books, 1970), 230, 231. Veblen first coined the term 'leisure class' in this work of 1899, to describe a social stratum – the *nouveaux riches* – who had been freed through financial means from labour, their success marked by conspicuous consumption. In *Pilgrimage* Mr Henderson aspires to such social standing

based on financial capital; Richardson's own father had sold the family grocery business in order to live the life of a gentleman on the invested proceeds. His bankruptcy resulted.

4. E. J. Hobsbawm, *The Age of Empire 1875–1914* (London: Sphere Books, 1989), 202.

5. Sarah Grand in *The Young Girl* (1898–9); quoted in Lucy Bland, 'The Married Woman, the "New woman" and the Feminist: Sexual Politics of the 1890s', in Jane Randall (ed.), *Equal or Different: Women's Politics 1800–1914* (Oxford: Blackwell, 1987), 145. Thanks to Joanne Winning for bringing this article to my attention.

6. Amy Lowell, *Men, Women and Ghosts*; cited in Andrew Thacker, 'Amy Lowell and H. D.: The Other Imagists', *Women: A Cultural Review*, 4/1 (1993), 54.

7. Virginia Woolf, 'Street Haunting: A London Adventure', in *Collected Essays*, iv (London: Hogarth Press, 1967), 156, 159, 165.

8. Rachel Bowlby, 'Walking, Women and Writing: Virginia Woolf as *Flâneuse*', in Isobel Armstrong (ed.), *New Feminist Discourses* (London: Routledge, 1992), 44, 43.

9. Virginia Woolf, 'Dorothy Richardson', in *Women and Writing*, 190.

10. Virginia Woolf, 'Memories of a Working Women's Guild', in Rachel Bowlby (ed.), *A Woman's Essays* (Harmondsworth: Penguin Books, 1992), 136.

11. Georg Lukács, *The Theory of the Novel*, trans. Anna Bostock (London: Merlin Press, 1978), 121–2.

12. Siegfried Kracauer, 'On Employment Exchanges'; cited in David Frisby, *Fragments of Modernity* (Cambridge: Polity Press, 1988), 144.

13. Theodor Herzl is the author of *The Jewish State* (1896), in which he argued for the resettlement of Jews in a state of their own. He is thus seen as the founder of the Zionist movement.

14. Peter Sloterdijk, *Critique of Cynical Reason*, trans. Michael Eldred with a Foreword by Andreas Huyssen (London: Verso Books, 1988), 6. Sloterdijk is identifying a condition he calls 'enlightened false consciousness', a 'cynical' form of modern borderline melancholia (p. 7) which is beyond susceptibility to the critique of ideology: 'It is that modernized, unhappy consciousness, on which enlightenment has laboured both successfully and in vain' (p. 5). Such a consciousness knows its falsity, but carries on nevertheless. The character of Miriam Henderson is not cynical in this sense. Yet the narrative of *Pilgrimage* comes earnestly close to representing the traces of such a condition, despite itself.

15. Arno J. Mayer, *Why did the Heavens not Darken: The 'Final Solution' in History* (London: Verso Books, 1990), 5.

16. Walter Benjamin, *One-Way Street*, trans. Edmund Jephcott and Kingsley Shorter (London: New Left Books, 1979), 89.

CHAPTER 4. MIRIORAMAS: FILM AND RICHARDSON

1. Bryher, *'Dawn's Left Hand'*, 338.
2. Ezra Pound, *Gaudier-Brzeska: A Memoir* (New York: New Directions Press, 1970), 89.
3. Richardson, quoted in Fromm, *Dorothy Richardson*, 173–4.
4. In this sense *Pilgrimage* becomes Miriam's own 'Song of Myself'. 'I loafe and invite my soul', as the voyaging ego of Whitman's poem puts it. *'You*, Miriam, are an incorrigeable *loafer'*, Hypo tells her (iii. 256). She reviews a 'bad little book on Whitman', as she tells him in *Revolving Lights* (iii. 369).
5. Theodor Adorno, 'Transparencies on Film'; quoted in Miriam Hansen, 'Mass Culture as Hieroglyphic Writing: Adorno, Derrida, Kracauer', *New German Critique*, 56 (1992), 69.
6. Béla Balázs, 'The Face of Man', from *Theory of the Film*, in Gerald Mast, Marshall Cohen, and Leo Braudy (eds.), *Film Theory and Criticism* (New York: Oxford University Press, 1992), 262.
7. Bryher, *'Dawn's Left Hand'*, 338.
8. For John Cowper Powys, in his *Dorothy Richardson*, she was 'a Wordsworth of the city of London; only she is a Wordsworth, who, in exchanging the mystery of mountains and lakes for the mystery of roof-tops and pavements, has purged away those teasing pedantries, puerilities and pieties which spoiled and cluttered up the great poet's original revelations' (19–20). Dorothy Richardson finds her home in, and celebrates the life of, the city: it is this that distinguishes her from such Romantic precursors.
9. Paul de Man, *Blindness and Insight: Essays in the Rhetoric of Contemporary Criticism* (London: Methuen, 1983), 46.
10. Judith Butler, *Bodies that Matter* (New York: Routledge, 1993), 162.
11. Eve Kosofsky Sedgwick, *Tendencies* (London: Routledge, 1994), 73.
12. Rebecca Egger, 'Deaf Ears and Dark Continents: Dorothy Richardson's Cinematic Epistemology', *Camera Obscura*, 30 (1992), 22. This useful article reads Richardson's construction of femininity alongside her response to racial difference and the coming of sound. While I am not sure that Richardson found cultural change as 'troubling' as Egger suggests – and read the politics of the encrypting of femininity and 'non-knowledge' rather differently – this excellent analysis of Richardson's conflation of technological and racial purity in her response to 'Dialogue in Dixie' (*CU6*) underlines contradictions also at work in the narrative of *Pilgrimage*, as I discussed earlier.
13. H.D. (Hilda Doolittle), 'Russian Films', *Close Up*, 3/3 (1928), 23. Richardson's opposition to English censorship might be seen as a protest against the 'impassable barriers' erected to prevent a fostering

of such internationalism. See 'The Censorship Petition', *Close Up* 6/1 (1930), 7–11.

14. Anne Friedberg, introducing Richardson's essay in *Framework* 20 (1982), 6–8; quoted in Miriam Hansen, *Babel and Babylon: Spectatorship in American Silent Film* (Cambridge, Mass.: Harvard University Press, 1991), 327.
15. Hansen, *Babel and Babylon*, 121.
16. Mary Ann Doane, *The Desire to Desire: The Woman's Film of the 1940s* (Bloomington, Ind.: Indiana University Press, 1987), 31.
17. Hansen, *Babel and Babylon*, 124.
18. Egger, 'Deaf Ears and Dark Continents', 9.
19. Hansen, *Babel and Babylon*, 125.

Select Bibliography

WORKS BY DOROTHY RICHARDSON

Pilgrimage (4 vols.; London: Virago, 1979). Original publication: *Pointed Roofs* (1915); *Backwater* (1916); *Honeycomb* (1917); *The Tunnel* (1919); *Interim* (1919); *Deadlock* (1921); *Revolving Lights* (1923); *The Trap* (1925); *Oberland* (1927); *Dawn's Left Hand* (1931); *Clear Horizon* (1935); *Dimple Hill* (1938); *March Moonlight* (1967).

Journey to Paradise, ed. Trudi Tate (London: Virago, 1989).

'Days with Walt Whitman', *Ye Crank*, 4 (1906), 259–63.

'The Garden' (1924); repr. in *Journey to Paradise*, 21–4.

'Women and the Future', *Vanity Fair*, 22 (1924), 39–40.

'Continuous Performance', *Close Up*, 1/1 (1927), 34–7.

'Continuous Performance: The Increasing Congregation', *Close Up*, 1/6 (1927), 61–5.

'Continuous Performance', *Close Up*, 2/3 (1928), 51–5.

'Continuous Performance: The Thoroughly Popular Film', *Close Up*, 2/4 (1928), 44–50.

'Continuous Performance: The Cinema in the Slums', *Close Up*, 2/5 (1928), 58–62.

'Mr Clive Bell's Proust', *New Adelphi*, 2/2 (1929), 160–2.

'Continuous Performance: Pictures and Films', *Close Up*, 4/1 (1929), 51–7.

'Continuous Performance: Dialogue in Dixie', *Close Up*, 5/3 (1929), 211–18.

'The Censorship Petition', *Close Up*, 6/1 (1930), 7–11.

'Continuous Performance: A Tear for Lycidas', *Close Up*, 7/3 (1930), 196–202.

'Continuous Performance: Narcissus', *Close Up*, 8/3 (1931), 182–5.

'Continuous Performance: This Spoon-Fed Generation?', *Close Up*, 8/4 (1931), 304–8.

'Continuous Performance: The Film Gone Male', *Close Up*, 9/1 (1932), 36–8.

'Beginnings' (1933); repr. in *Journey to Paradise*, 110–13.

BIOGRAPHICAL AND CRITICAL STUDIES

Blake, Caeser, *Dorothy Richardson* (Ann Arbor, Mich.: University of Michigan Press, 1960). Earliest biography of Richardson, often sensationalist and unsympathetic in its detail.

Blau, DuPlessis, Rachel, 'Beyond the Hard Visible Horizon', in *Writing Beyond the Ending: Narrative Strategies of Twentieth-Century Women Writers* (Bloomington, Ind.: Indiana University Press, 1985), 142–61. Good on Richardson's representation of sexuality, and on the quest narrative, which she compares with Zora Neale Hurston's *Their Eyes were Watching God*.

Bryher, Winifred, *'Dawn's Left Hand'*, *Close Up*, 8/4 (1931), 337–8. Review of Richardson's volume which makes claims for her novel as the English film 'for which many are waiting'.

Egger, Rebecca, 'Deaf Ears and Dark Continents: Dorothy Richardson's Cinematic Epistemology', *Camera Obscura*, 30 (1992), 5–33. Useful reading of Richardson's *Close Up* column, particularly sharp on her representation of racial difference.

[Fromm] Glikin, Gloria, 'Dorothy Richardson; The Personal "Pilgrimage"', *PMLA* 78 (1963), 586–600. Examines the correspondences between life and work.

—— 'Variations on a Method', *James Joyce Quarterly*, 2/1 (1964), 42–9. Comparison of Richardson and Joyce which places her work in a wider modernist context.

Fromm, Gloria, *Dorothy Richardson: A Biography* (Urbana, Ill.: University of Illinois Press, 1977). The most comprehensive biography of Richardson, which gives a real sense of the complications and hardships she experienced, and the relationship between the text and the life. Full bibliography of Richardson's extensive writings.

Hanscombe, Gillian, *The Art of Life: Dorothy Richardson and the Development of Feminist Consciousness* (London: Peter Owen, 1982). Useful study of Richardson as a female and feminist writer, and what it might mean to describe her as such in a modernist context.

Heath, Stephen, 'Writing for Silence: Dorothy Richardson and the Novel', in Susanne Kappeler and Norman Bryson (eds.), *Teaching the Text* (London: Routledge & Kegan Paul, 1983), 126–47. Excellent reading of the nature of Richardson's writing of 'the feminine', alive to its specificity and to its context.

Hyde, Lawrence, 'The Work of Dorothy Richardson', *Adelphi* 2 (1924), 508–17. Critical engagement with Richardson's work which argues, against Beresford and Sinclair, that the novel is superficial and, in aesthetic terms, a failure.

Kumar, Shiv K., 'Dorothy Richardson and the Dilemma of "Being versus Becoming" ', *Modern Language Notes*, 74 (1959), 494-501. Brief reading of Richardson's novel in terms of the Bergson of *The Creative Mind*.

Labovitz, Esther Kleinbord, *The Myth of the Heroine: The Female Bildingsroman in the Twentieth Century* (New York: Peter Lang, 1986). Miriam's 'pilgrimage toward self-realization' is placed usefully within the tradition of the *Bildungsroman*.

Levy, Anita, 'Gendered Labor, the Woman Writer and Dorothy Richardson', *Novel: A Forum on Fiction*, 25/1 (1991), 50–70. Interesting reading of *Pilgrimage* in terms of the representation and gendering of the working woman as intellectual.

Powys, John Cowper, *Dorothy M. Richardson* (London: Village Press, 1974). First published 1931. Rather hyperbolic celebration of Richardson's work and the 'lost Atlantis of feminine susceptibility' that she uncovers, by one of her own generation.

Radford, Jean, *Dorothy Richardson* (Hemel Hempstead: Harvester Wheatsheaf, 1991). A good introduction to *Pilgrimage* which suggestively reads Richardson as a precursor of *écriture feminine*.

Rose, Shirley, 'The Unmoving Center: Consciousness in Dorothy Richardson's *Pilgrimage*', *Contemporary Literature*, 10/3 (1969), 366–82. Useful discussion of the inappropriateness of the notion of 'stream of consciousness' to Richardson's narrative.

Rosenberg, John, *Dorothy Richardson: The Genius they Forgot* (London: Gerald Duckworth & Co Ltd, 1973). Written to commemorate the centenary of her birth, this is a rather traditional account of an 'author's life'.

Sinclair, May, 'The Novels of Dorothy Richardson', in Bonnie Kime Scott (ed.), *The Gender of Modernism* (Bloomington, Ind.: Indiana University Press, 1990), 442–8. Originally published in the *Egoist* in 1918, this influential article applies William James's notion of 'stream of consciousness' to Richardson's narrative.

Staley, Thomas, *Dorothy Richardson* (Boston: Twayne Publishers, 1976). Factually accurate representation of Richardson's life which avoids the more complicated issues.

Trickett, Rachel, 'The Living Dead – V: Dorothy Richardson', *London Magazine*, 6/6 (1959), 20–5. Appears to take on the terms of Woolf's 'Women and Fiction' essay in arguing that Richardson is a propagandist for 'the woman's outlook' like Charlotte Brontë while Woolf's more impersonal style 'is a measure of her superiority'.

Watts, Carol, 'Releasing Possibility into Form: Cultural Choice and the Women Writer', in Isobel Armstrong (ed.), *New Feminist Discourses* (London: Routledge, 1992), 83–102. Reads the aesthetic form of *Pilgrimage* and its representation of gendered identity in terms of a feminist cultural materialism.

Woolf, Virginia, 'Dorothy Richardson', in Michèle Barrett (ed.), *Virginia Woolf: Women and Writing* (London: Women's Press, 1979), 188–192. Useful reprinting of Woolf's reviews of *The Tunnel* and *Revolving Lights*, including her famous statement on Richardson's invention of 'the psychological sentence of the feminine gender'.

BACKGROUND READING

Adorno, Theodor, 'Short Commentaries on Proust', in *Notes to Literature*, i, ed. Rolf Tiedemann, trans. Shierry Weber Nicholsen (New York: Columbia University Press, 1991), 174–84.

Barthes, Roland, *Camera Lucida: Reflections on Photography*, trans. Richard Howard (London: Fontana, 1984).

Balázs, Béla, 'The Face of Man' from *Theory of the Film*, in Gerald Mast, Marshall Cohen, and Leo Brady (eds.), *Film Theory and Criticism* (New York: Oxford University Press, 1992), 260–7.

Benjamin, Walter, *Illuminations*, ed. Hannah Arendt, trans. Harry Zohn (London: Fontana/Collins, 1973).

—— *One-way Street*, trans. Edmund Jephcott and Kingsley Shorter (London: New Left Books, 1979).

Bland, Lucy, 'The Married Woman, the "New Woman" and the Feminist: Sexual Politics of the 1890s', in Jane Randall (ed.), *Equal or Different: Women's Politics 1800–1914* (Oxford: Blackwell, 1987), 141–63.

Bowlby, Rachel, 'Walking, Women and Writing: Virginia Woolf as *flâneuse*', in Isobel Armstrong, (ed.), *New Feminist Discourses* (London: Routledge, 1992), 26–47.

Buck-Morss, Susan, *The Dialectics of Seeing: Walter Benjamin and the Arcades Project* (Cambridge, Mass.: MIT Press, 1989).

Butler, Judith, *Bodies that Matter* (New York and London: Routledge, 1993).

De Man, Paul, *Blindness and Insight: Essays in the Rhetoric of Contemporary Criticism* (London: Methuen, 1983).

Doane, Mary Ann, *The Desire to Desire: The Woman's Film of the 1940s* (Bloomington, Ind.: Indiana University Press, 1987).

Foucault, Michel, 'Of Other Spaces', *Diacritics*, 16/1 (1986), 23–7.

Freud, Sigmund, 'Beyond the Pleasure Principle', in *On Metapsychology* (Harmondsworth: Penguin, 1991), 269–338.

—— 'Childhood Memories and Screen Memories', in *The Psychopathology of Everyday Life*, standard edn., vi; (London: Hogarth Press, 1960), 43–52.

Green, André, 'The Dead Mother', in his *On Private Madness* (London: Hogarth Press and Institute of Psychoanalysis, 1986), 142–73.

Hanscombe, Gillian, and Smyers, Virginia, *Writing for their Lives* (London: Women's Press, 1988).

Hansen, Miriam, *Babel and Babylon: Spectatorship in American Silent Film* (Cambridge, Mass.: Harvard University Press, 1991).

H. D., 'Russian Films', *Close Up*, 3/3 (1928), 18–29.

Hobsbawm, E. J., *The Age of Empire 1875–1914* (London: Sphere Books, 1989).

Jameson, Fredric, *Modernism and Imperialism* (Derry: Field Day, 1988).

Kracauer, Siegfried, 'Photography', trans. Thomas Y. Levin, *Critical Inquiry*, 19 (1993), 421–36.

Krauss, Rosalind, 'A Note on Photography and the Simulacral', *October*, 31 (1984), 49–68.

—— *The Optical Unconscious* (Cambridge, Mass.: MIT Press, 1993).

Kristeva, Julia, *Proust and the Sense of Time*, trans. Stephen Bann (London: Faber and Faber, 1993).

Mayer, Arno J., *Why did the Heavens not Darken: The 'Final Solution' in History* (London: Verso Books, 1990).

Raitt, Suzanne, *Vita and Virginia: The Work and Friendship of Vita Sackville-West and Virginia Woolf* (Oxford: Clarendon Press, 1993).

Scott, Bonnie Kime, (ed.), *The Gender of Modernism* (Bloomington, Ind.: Indiana University Press, 1990).

Sedgwick, Eve Kosofsky, *Tendencies* (London: Routledge, 1994).

Sloterdijk, Peter, *Critique of Cynical Reason*, trans. Michael Eldred (London: Verso Books, 1988).

Thacker, Andrew, 'Amy Lowell and H. D.: The Other Imagists', *Women: A Cultural Review*, 4/1 (1993), 49–59.

Veblen, Thorstein, T*he Theory of the Leisure Class: An Economic Study of Institutions* (London: Unwin Books, 1970).

Williams, Raymond, *The English Novel from Dickens to Lawrence* (London: Chatto & Windus, 1973).

Woolf, Virginia, 'Memories of a Working Women's Guild', in Rachel Bowlby (ed.), *A Woman's Essays* (Harmondsworth: Penguin Books, 1992), 133–47.

—— 'Street Haunting: A London Adventure', in *Collected Essays*, iv (London: Hogarth Press, 1967), 155–66.

—— *Women and Writing*, ed. Michèle Barrett (London: Women's Press, 1979).

—— *A Writer's Diary*, ed. Leonard Woolf (London: Hogarth Press, 1959).

Index

*Recent and
Forthcoming Titles
in the
New Series of*

WRITERS AND
THEIR WORK

─────────────

WRITERS AND THEIR WORK

RECENT & FORTHCOMING TITLES

Title	Author
Aphra Behn	*Sue Wiseman*
Angela Carter	*Lorna Sage*
John Clare	*John Lucas*
Joseph Conrad	*Cedric Watts*
John Donne	*Stevie Davies*
Henry Fielding	*Jenny Uglow*
Elizabeth Gaskell	*Kate Flint*
William Golding	*Kevin McCarron*
William Hazlitt	*J.B. Priestley; R.L. Brett (introduction by Michael Foot)*
George Herbert	*T.S. Eliot (introduction by Peter Porter)*
Henry James - The Later Writing	*Barbara Hardy*
King Lear	*Terence Hawkes*
Doris Lessing	*Elizabeth Maslen*
Children's Literature	*Kimberley Reynolds*
David Lodge	*Bernard Bergonzi*
Christopher Marlowe	*Thomas Healy*
Andrew Marvell	*Annabel Patterson*
Ian McEwan	*Kiernan Ryan*
Walter Pater	*Laurel Brake*
Jean Rhys	*Helen Carr*
Dorothy Richardson	*Carol Watts*
The Sensation Novel	*Lyn Pykett*

TITLES IN PREPARATION

Title	Author
Antony and Cleopatra	*Ken Parker*
W.H. Auden	*Stan Smith*
Jane Austen	*Robert Clark*
A.S. Byatt	*Richard Todd*
Lord Byron	*J. Drummond Bone*
Geoffrey Chaucer	*Steve Ellis*
Coleridge	*Stephen Bygrave*
Charles Dickens	*Rod Mengham*
George Eliot	*Josephine McDonagh*
Brian Friel	*Geraldine Higgins*
Graham Greene	*Peter Mudford*
Hamlet	*Ann Thompson & Neil Taylor*
Thomas Hardy	*Peter Widdowson*
David Hare	*Jeremy Ridgman*
Tony Harrison	*Joe Kelleher*
Seamus Heaney	*Andrew Murphy*
James Joyce	*Steven Connor*
Rudyard Kipling	*Jan Montefiore*

TITLES IN PREPARATION

Title	Author
Franz Kafka	*Michael Wood*
D.H. Lawrence	*Linda Ruth Williams*
A Midsummer Night's Dream	*Helen Hackett*
Brian Patten	*Linda Cookson*
Alexander Pope	*Pat Rogers*
Sylvia Plath	*Elizabeth Bronfen*
Salman Rushdie	*Damian Grant*
Sir Walter Scott	*John Sutherland*
Edmund Spenser	*Colin Burrow*
Jonathan Swift	*Claude Rawson*
The Tempest	*Gordon McMullan*
J.R.R. Tolkien	*Charles Moseley*
Leo Tolstoy	*John Bayley*
Mary Wollstonecraft	*Jane Moore*
Evelyn Waugh	*Malcolm Bradbury*
Angus Wilson	*Peter Conradi*
Virginia Woolf	*Laura Marcus*
William Wordsworth	*Nicholas Roe*
Working Class Fiction	*Ian Haywood*
Charlotte Yonge	*Alethea Hayter*